IMAGES
of America

SUN VALLEY,
KETCHUM, AND THE
WOOD RIVER VALLEY

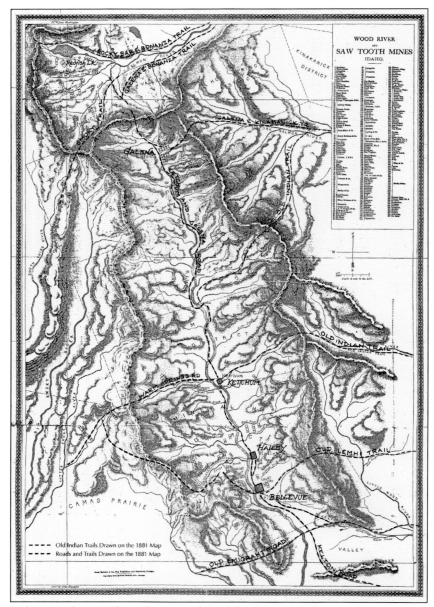

This map shows Indian trails and mines of the Wood River Valley in 1881. Natives used the Old Lemhi Trail to travel from Montana's Lemhi Valley to Bellevue then on to Camas Prairie to harvest camas roots. The Ole Emigrant Trail (the Oregon Trail's Goodale's Cutoff) left the main trail near Fort Hall and joined it again at Mountain Home. The Kelton Road connected the valley to the Union Pacific Railroad at Kelton, Utah. (Courtesy Evelyn Phillips.)

ON THE COVER: Sun Valley Resort was Union Pacific board chairman Averell Harriman's creation to stimulate rail passenger traffic decimated by the Depression. Opened in December 1936 at a cost of $1.5 million, it was the country's first destination ski resort and a magnet for beautiful people and serious skiers. This publicity photograph shows the activities available at the resort. (Courtesy the Community Library.)

IMAGES
of America

SUN VALLEY,
KETCHUM, AND THE
WOOD RIVER VALLEY

John W. Lundin

ARCADIA
PUBLISHING

Published by Arcadia Publishing
Charleston, South Carolina

Printed in the United States of America

Library of Congress Control Number: 2019957391

For all general information, please contact Arcadia Publishing:
Telephone 843-853-2070
Fax 843-853-0044
E-mail sales@arcadiapublishing.com
For customer service and orders:
Toll-Free 1-888-313-2665

Visit us on the Internet at www.arcadiapublishing.com

This book is dedicated to the hardy pioneers who settled Idaho's Wood River Valley in the 1880s, including the author's great-grandparents Matt and Isabelle Campbell McFall. In 1881, it took them two weeks of hard travel from Eureka, Nevada, to reach this remote, mountainous outpost. They stayed and thrived, helping to lay the foundation for what the area has become.

CONTENTS

ACKNOWLEDGMENTS

This book was written for the Center for Regional History of the Community Library in Ketchum, Idaho, which will receive the author's proceeds. The center has over 14,000 historic photographs, along with Union Pacific materials obtained after the railroad sold Sun Valley to the Janss Company in 1964.

Thanks go to a number of people for their help, including Mary Tyson, the center's director, and Ryan Gelskey and Nicole Potter for preparing photographs. Thanks also to the Idaho State Historical Society, the Mary Jane Griffith family, the Zentmeyer family, the Idaho Department of Parks and Recreation, Bud Purdy and Alan Engen for the use of their pictures, and Evelyn Phillips for the use of her maps. Unless otherwise noted, photographs in this book appear courtesy of the Community Library.

There are few pictures of Hailey in this book, since the Images of America book *Hailey*, by Robert A. Lonning, was published in 2012.

John W. Lundin is an attorney, historian, and author who has written extensively about Washington and Idaho history. His great-grandparents, Matt and Isabelle Campbell McFall, moved to Bellevue, Idaho, in 1881 for the silver strike and were pioneers in the Wood River Valley. Lundin's papers about Wood River Valley history can be found at the Center for Regional History. His essays on Washington history are published on HistoryLink.org, the online encyclopedia of Washington history. In 2018, his book *Early Skiing on Snoqualmie Pass* received an award as an outstanding regional ski history book from the International Ski History Association. His book *Skiing Sun Valley: A History from Union Pacific to the Holdings* will be published by The History Press in 2020. John learned to ski using wooden skis, cable bindings, leather boots, and rope tows. He first skied in Sun Valley in 1960 after a 24-hour train ride from Seattle, when a one-week pass cost $39. John is a founder of the Washington State Ski & Snowboard Museum. His website is www.johnwlundin.com.

INTRODUCTION

The announcement in summer 2019 of an archaeological find at Cooper's Ferry in western Idaho, at the junction of Rock Creek and the lower Salmon River, indicated that humans arrived in North America 16,000 years ago, likely traveling by boat from Asia along the Pacific coast, then going up the Columbia River to the Snake and Salmon Rivers. The site has the continent's earliest radiocarbon-dated evidence of people interacting with extinct animals. Early people hunted and fished in Idaho's Snake River Valley 14,000 years ago. In 1989, an 11,000-year-old woman's skeleton was found near Buhl, Idaho. Native Americans traveled through the Wood River Valley for thousands of years to fish, hunt, and harvest food in nearby areas, including Camas Prairie, where they obtained camas roots. In 1961, a deposit of Clovis tools was found on Camas Prairie near Fairfield dating to around 10,000 BC. In 1972, a Clovis tool manufacturing site 6,000 to 10,000 years old was discovered at Elkhorn in Sun Valley.

Alexander Ross was the first white known to have visited the Wood River Valley. In the 1820s, Ross led a Pacific Fur Company party that trapped beaver and looked for new territory. Starting in Montana, Ross's party explored along the Salmon, Big Lost, and Big Wood Rivers. He crossed the Galena Summit on September 18, 1824.

From 1843 to the 1850s, between 250,000 and 350,000 people traveled west on the Oregon Trail, going through Idaho to Oregon's Willamette Valley, the 1849 California Gold Rush, and Puget Sound. Travel through Idaho's Snake River Valley was unpleasant, and few migrants stayed. Goodale's Cutoff was used after 1862 to avoid "Indian trouble" along the main route. It went northwest from Fort Hall in eastern Idaho, past the present city of Arco, across the Big Wood River, and through Camas Prairie, rejoining the main trail near Mountain Home.

Mining brought the first whites to settle in Idaho. In the winter of 1860, gold was discovered on the Clearwater Branch of the Snake River, attracting 5,000 prospectors by the summer of 1861. More gold was found on the South Fork of the Clearwater River and the Salmon River basin in 1861 and in the Boise River basin in 1862. In 1863, there was a gold rush to the South Boise River area, and mining camps opened in Leesburg, Stanley, Atlanta, and Rocky Bar. On March 3, 1863, Congress formed Idaho Territory by splitting "that portion of Washington [Territory] . . . east of Oregon and the 117th meridian of west longitude," including what later became Montana Territory. Lewiston was the first territorial capital, but it was moved to Boise City in December 1864. In 1864, Montana Territory was created, and in 1868, Wyoming Territory was formed, taking the Yellowstone area and Teton Mountains from Idaho Territory.

In 1864, gold was discovered on the southwest edge of Camas Prairie (the Camas Gold Belt), 11 miles from the future town of Hailey, attracting prospectors who disturbed Native Americans' annual spring camas harvests. Galena ore was found where Goodale's Cutoff crossed the Big Wood River, although it was not mined, since prospectors were searching for gold. In 1866, gold was discovered on the Yankee Fork of the Salmon River, but problems with local Indian tribes prevented large-scale mining operations from starting.

The Bannock War of 1878 was the result of a decade of increasing tensions between whites and Indians on Camas Prairie. The government's failure to provide Bannocks living on the Fort Hall Reservation the supplies they were promised exacerbated historic conflicts, and the seizure of Bannock horses led to an uprising on Camas Prairie in 1878. Army forces defeated the Bannock band, who were returned to their reservation, opening the way for settlement of the Wood River Valley.

The Wood River Valley experienced several economic eras since whites first began settling here in 1879, a rollercoaster ride of boom-bust cycles influenced by national and international events. Until the 1960s, the valley's economy depended on its railroad connection to the outside world. The valley's economy was initially based on mining galena ore (an amalgam of silver, lead, and zinc), leading to a silver boom in the early 1880s. In 1883, the Wood River Branch of the Oregon Short Line Railroad (a Union Pacific subsidiary) was built from Shoshone to Hailey, connecting this remote valley to the outside world, bringing in outside capital and modern technology and causing an economic boom. In 1888, the international silver depression shut down the country's mining industry. In Idaho, mining was replaced by sheep raising and agriculture, stimulated by the Desert Land Act of 1894 and the Reclamation Act of 1902, an economic era lasting through World War I. Idaho was hit hard by an agricultural depression in the 1920s, made worse by the Great Depression starting in 1929. The valley's last economic era began in 1936, when Union Pacific board chairman Averell Harriman built a ski resort for $1.5 million (nearly $28 million today) in the remote mountains of Idaho to stimulate rail passenger service, which had been decimated by the Depression. Known as America's St. Moritz, Sun Valley was the country's first destination ski resort. It became an international destination, and began modern skiing in this country.

One

WOOD RIVER VALLEY'S MINING ORIGINS

In 1878, the Wood River region "was in the control of the Indians and threats from the Bannocks deterred prospectors," according to Clark C. Spence in *For Wood River or Bust*. By the late 1870s, new methods of smelting galena ore developed in Eureka, Nevada, along with settlement of the Bannock uprising, made the valley's ore attractive and opened the valley to prospectors.

In 1879, prospectors made a number of productive finds in the Wood River Valley. David Ketchum found galena ore at the headwaters of the Big Wood River in May, and Warren Callahan filed the valley's first formal claim for the Galena Mine. Claims were recorded for finds in Galena Gulch west of Bellevue for the Queen of the Hills, Wood River, and Penobscot Mines. By the summer of 1879, more than a dozen mines were operating. By September, 230 claims had been filed, and the Wood River Mining District was formed to establish rules for recording and regulating claims. By the end of 1879, there were 342 mining locations, and 12 mines were purchased by outside investors for $100,000.

Word of the valley's riches reached the outside world, and many thousands of hopefuls poured in to seek their fortunes. In 1879 and 1880, two thousand claims were filed. Valley mines produced over $1 million in ore in 1881, most shipped by wagon to railheads and then to smelters in Omaha, Salt Lake, Kansas City, or Denver for processing, yielding from $100 to $500 per ton in silver.

The Wood River Valley was remote and isolated. Everything traveled by stagecoach or wagon. Concord coaches pulled by six horses carried mail, freight, and seven passengers facing each other. The valley was connected to the outside world by two wagon roads. A 135-mile road led to the Utah & Northern Railroad stop at Blackfoot, Idaho, between Idaho Falls and Pocatello. (The Utah & Northern was a Union Pacific subsidiary connecting Ogden, Utah, with Butte, Montana.) A 170-mile road led to Kelton, Utah, a seven-day trip connecting with the Union Pacific's transcontinental line. Stages linked the valley's towns with each other from Bellevue north to Galena and with outlying mining districts. A road from Bellevue running east through Muldoon Canyon led to the mining community of Muldoon in the Little Wood Valley. A road from Hailey connected with mining communities in Croy Canyon. In the summer of 1881, a toll road was built over the Galena Summit to the Sawtooth Valley. In 1883, a road was built west from Ketchum along Warm Springs Creek to the Smoky Mining Districts over the Dollarhide Summit.

Before the valley's mines could be fully developed, smelters were needed to separate the silver and lead from the ore and remove impurities, and smelters required large capital investments. The silver boom soon attracted outside capitalists. The Philadelphia Smelter opened in October 1881, built for $500,000 (nearly $12 million today) by investors from Philadelphia, on a 160-acre bench at the head of Warm Springs Canyon. The smelter brought the latest technology, including an electric lighting system, by the fall of 1882. By that year, $1.5 million had been invested in valley mines, which were responsible for one third of Idaho's total gold and silver production, valued at $3.5 million, and there were 14 major sales of mining property.

The Wood River Valley's silver-lead belt was "one of the richest as well as one of the most extensive in the world . . . extending from Bellevue to Ketchum, and [was] only part of the silver-bearing region which comprised between 4,000 and 5,000 square miles," according to Hubert Howe Bancroft's *History of Washington, Idaho and Montana*. The valley was the "best mining camp ever seen in this country at this age." The *Wood River News-Miner* noted on August 5, 1882:

> The mining and milling companies are just now starting in to make a showing for Wood River, and its yield of $1,000,000 last year will go to $3,000,000 this year. This is better than Leadville in Colorado, Butte in Montana, Tombstone in Arizona, or Eureka in Nevada, did at the same age, although they were better situated as to transportation and smelting facilities.

Beginning in 1879, thousands of hopefuls poured into the Wood River Valley seeking their fortunes, carrying their supplies on mules. By the summer of 1880, two thousand claims were filed, and between 3,500 and 5,000 people lived in the valley. (Photograph by Eugene Antz.)

Prospectors engaged in "pick and shovel" mining, involving hard manual labor that required little capital, but they were only able to access ore close to the surface. Many sold their claims to outsiders with financial resources to exploit those claims. (Courtesy the Idaho State Historical Society.)

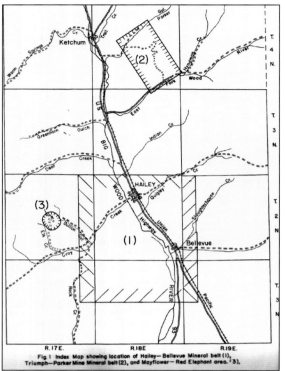

Three mining districts were established in September 1879 to set rules for recording and regulating claims: Hailey-Bellevue Mineral Belt, containing Galena Gulch west of Bellevue and areas around Hailey; Parker Mineral Belt, between East Fork and Elkhorn; and Mayflower–Red Elephant in Croy Canyon. This map is from *Detailed Geology of Certain Areas in the Mineral Hill and Warm Springs Mining Districts* by the Idaho Bureau of Mines and Geology.

The Wood River Valley was isolated in the early 1880s. Stagecoaches and wagons provided connections with two railroad towns. The first was to Blackfoot in eastern Idaho (135 miles), with a station of the Utah & Northern (a Union Pacific subsidiary), going from Ogden, Utah, to Butte, Montana. The second was to Kelton, (160 miles) on the Union Pacific's main line. Wagons took seven days to travel from Kelton to Hailey, and stages took 42 hours.

Fig. 1 Index Map showing location of Hailey—Bellevue Mineral belt (1), Triumph—Parker Mine Mineral belt (2), and Mayflower—Red Elephant area. (3).

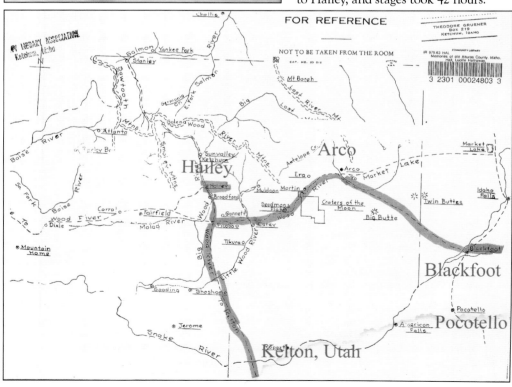

Wagons pulled by mules or oxen transported goods in and out of the valley. In July 1881, the valley's first shipment of 22,000 pounds of bullion was transported by six wagons to Blackfoot for shipment by rail to Omaha, Nebraska, for smelting at a cost of $90 per ton.

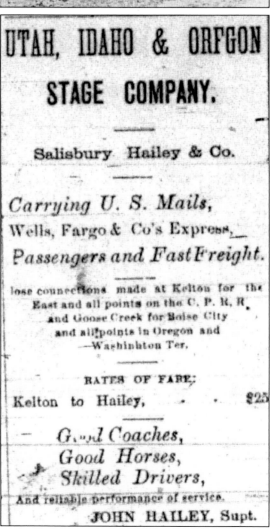

Stagecoach lines carried mail, passengers, and freight. John Hailey's stage line ran between Kelton, Boise City, and the valley. Gilmer & Salisbury operated stages to the valley from rail stops at Blackfoot and Kelton. Stages connected valley towns to each other and to nearby mining districts. This advertisement is from the *Wood River Times* of May 5, 1883.

13

According to Carrie Adell Strahorn's *Fifteen Thousand Miles by Stage*, three stages a day began arriving in the valley in the spring of 1881, "fairly groaning under their weight of live freight," bringing 75 to 100 newcomers. Reservations had to be made several days in advance. The cost from Boise to Hailey was $22.50 and from Kelton to Hailey $25. Meals cost $1, and it cost 75¢ to sleep on the floor of a log cabin.

The Philadelphia Smelter opened in the fall of 1881, built for $500,000 (nearly $12 million today) by investors from Philadelphia, on a 160-acre bench at the head of Warm Springs Canyon. It had two 40-ton furnaces to remove impurities and separate galena ore into silver, lead, and zinc.

PHILADELPHIA SMELTERS, NEAR KETCHUM, ALTURAS CO. IDAHO, PROPERTY OF THE PHILADELPHIA MINING & SMELTING CO.

This illustration from the 1884 *History of Idaho Territory: Showing its Resources and Advantages* depicts the Philadelphia Smelter, its buildings, and 20 kilns to burn wood to make charcoal for its furnaces. The smelter ended up processing most of the ore in the Wood River Valley and surrounding mining districts.

Timber was in great demand. The mining industry needed timbers to support underground workings, lumber was needed for buildings, and the railroad needed wood for railroad ties. F. Young's sawmill at North Fork is seen here.

Horses and oxen were used in logging operations. Here, horses drag logs from where they were cut to a sawmill.

Oxen haul logs through Ketchum. The Comstock & Clark building is behind the wagon, and Isaac I. Lewis's First National Bank of Ketchum is on the right.

Two

EARLY SETTLEMENT

Beginning in the spring of 1880, prospectors from all over the world seeking their fortunes flooded into the "wonderful Wood River country." The Silver City *Owyhee Avalanche* of July 23, 1881, described the area:

> [Its] natural advantages and attractions were seldom . . . surpassed by any mining region; the country is easy of access; wood and water are plentiful; water power for machinery can be procured almost anywhere; . . . the climate, during the summer months, is delightful, . . . the winters are not extremely cold . . . game of all kinds is to be met with in abundance . . . and the scenery in the mountains is grand and picturesque beyond description.

In May 1880, Bellevue was surveyed by John Walker, Bill Seaman, and A.Y. Hash, and 300 inches of water were claimed from Seamands Creek in Muldoon Canyon for its water supply. Bellevue got a post office in June 1880 and had 2,000 residents by the fall of 1881. By the fall of 1882, the town had a daily newspaper, nine saloons, four churches, three blacksmiths, three hotels, seven attorneys, four physicians, three assayers, a wide variety of merchants, and "the best race track in the northwest," according to the *Bellevue Chronicle*. Farms in the Bellevue Triangle south of town had the valley's best water and soil and produced food for the growing communities. Bellevue was the valley's "Gate City."

In 1879, John Hailey filed a Homestead Act claim for the townsite of Hailey, and in 1880, Hailey, W.T. Riley, E.S. Chase, and A.H. Boomer consolidated their land claims to 440 acres and formed the Hailey Town Company. In April 1881, five hundred inches of water from Indian Creek was claimed for the town's water supply, and in May, the town was officially platted. In 1881, Hailey had a population of 2,700 housed in tents, 75 buildings, and 5 saloons where "first class liquor is sold at two bits a drink," according to *For Wood River or Bust*. Hailey became the county seat for Alturas County, narrowly defeating Bellevue in a contested election. In 1882, the Idaho & Oregon Land Improvement Company, whose owners were affiliated with the Oregon Short Line Railroad, purchased the townsites of Shoshone and Hailey, knowing that a branch line would be built connecting them. In 1883, the company filed for 12,000 inches of Big Wood River water and dug a canal to irrigate land south of Hailey.

On May 2, 1880, Isaac Ives (I.I.) Lewis and Albert Griffith platted a new town 13 miles north of Hailey and named it after early explorer David Ketchum. Lewis filed for 200 inches of water from Trail Creek for the town's water supply. Mary Jane Griffith wrote in *Early History of Ketchum and Sun Valley* that "Ketchum literally exploded—thousands of men poured in over a mere few weeks, each eager settler seeking a new life in this land of opportunity."

The Lewis family played a key role in the valley's development. I.I. Lewis was Ketchum's first assayer, owned a cattle ranch, had interests in several mercantile operations and a number of mines, operated the newspaper *Ketchum Keystone*, and formed the First National Bank of Ketchum and the Ketchum Water Supply Company.

Thousands of immigrants filled valley towns with a chaos of activity, described in *For Wood River or Bust*:

> All was hustle and bustle: action punctuated by braying pack animals and genuine frontier language, loudly and impiously spoken. All day long, and far into the night . . . men from every quarter of the globe, bronzed and bearded miners, merchants, professional men, uncouth bullwhackers, profane mule skinners, quartz experts, stock sharps, gamblers and desperados crowd the sidewalks and throng the saloons.

Drinking and gambling were central parts of life. Saloons, dancehalls, gamblers, and female beer-jerkers kept the towns lively. Prostitution thrived, and every town had its "sporting district" with "single men's wives." Hailey was described by a St. Louis paper:

> Newspapers make no bones of fist fights, and officers are instructed to make no arrests unless weapons are called into requisition. Only shooting and cutting scrapes attract more than passing attention. A fist fight is of about as much importance as a street dog fight. . . . Saloons and kindred places of amusement are open night and day, and business is fully as good at 4 a.m. as at 4 p.m.

Isaac Ives Lewis, a banker from Butte, Montana, arrived in the valley with Al Griffith in May 1880, and with George McCoy, surveyed and platted the Ketchum townsite, becoming known as Ketchum's founder. He became wealthy through investments in real estate and mines, ran several businesses, owned Ketchum's newspaper, opened the First National Bank of Ketchum, and provided the town with water.

Isaac and Georgeanna Lewis (shown here in 1895) had three boys (Horace, George, and Clancey) and two daughters (Gertrude and Mary). After her husband made a fortune in the valley, Georgeanna traveled extensively and purchased land in Minnesota, Florida, and Seattle.

The Lewis Ranch along Trail Creek is pictured, with Ketchum in the background. The Brass family owned the ranch in 1936 when it was purchased by the Union Pacific for the Sun Valley Resort.

Hot springs on Warm Springs Creek were used for bathhouses, including this one owned by the Lewis family, another owned by the Philadelphia Smelter for its employees, and one for Guyer Hot Springs Resort.

Al Griffith arrived in Ketchum with I.I. Lewis in May 1880. He worked as a mine foreman, and in 1887, operated a store in the Smoky Mining District. His house in Ketchum still stands at East and Sixth Streets. His sons Albert and Oscar opened Griffith Grocery on Ketchum's Main Street where the Cornerstone Restaurant was recently located. (Courtesy Mary Jane Griffith family.)

George and Sarah McCoy moved to the Wood River Valley in November 1880 with their seven children (shown here in 1890). They built a cabin and survived a harsh winter, eventually raising cattle and hay on their homestead south of Ketchum. Sarah became known as "Grandma McCoy."

The McCoy homestead, located just south of Ketchum's city limits, is now Reinheimer Ranch. This is its informal entrance. The ranch was bought in 1941 by Howard Reinheimer, a New York attorney, and was donated to the Idaho Park Foundation in 1976. Its white barn on the west side of Highway 75 is recognizable by its wagon-wheel window.

Sid Venable was an early settler in Ketchum who owned the Venable Livery Stable on Main Street. His house is now the Kneadery on Leadville Avenue.

This view of Ketchum from the 1880s looks northwest toward the Big Wood River and Bald Mountain. The multistory buildings are the Ketchum School (near center) and the Comstock & Clark building on what later became Sun Valley Road.

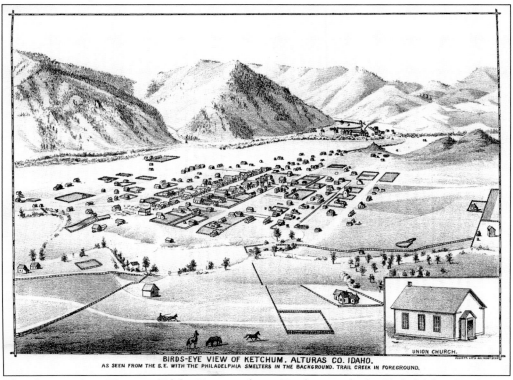

BIRDS-EYE VIEW OF KETCHUM. ALTURAS CO. IDAHO.
AS SEEN FROM THE S.E. WITH THE PHILADELPHIA SMELTERS IN THE BACKGROUND. TRAIL CREEK IN FOREGROUND.

UNION CHURCH.

This drawing from *History of Idaho Territory* shows Ketchum with the Philadelphia Smelter in the background at the head of Warm Springs Canyon.

Ketchum's Swift & Regan General Merchandise and Mining Supplies sold powder, fuse, and steel for miners; clothing, groceries, and provisions of all kinds; and was a wholesale dealer in liquors, wines, and fine cigars.

Ketchum's Assay Office and Wood River Market are seen here with the Comstock & Clark building in the background. Assayers were critical to the mining industry. They determined the mineral contents of ore, since smelting techniques differed based on the precise combination of minerals and impurities.

This was Ketchum's newspaper and job office. Each town's newspaper promoted its interests. The valley had 14 newspapers over the years, some publishing daily and some weekly, some supporting Democrats and others supporting Republicans. The *Ketchum Keystone* was published from 1882 to 1899.

Drinking was one of the few recreational activities available in the valley's early days, and every town had multiple saloons that served as social clubs. Here, the boys on the porch of Ketchum's Reed Saloon enjoy their beverage of choice.

Wood River Valley was originally in Alturas County. Prospectors had to travel 85 miles to Rocky Bar, the county seat, to register mining claims. In 1882, Hailey defeated Bellevue in a hotly contested election to become the new county seat, gaining political and economic power. The Alturas County Courthouse was built in Hailey in 1884. Blaine County was created in 1895.

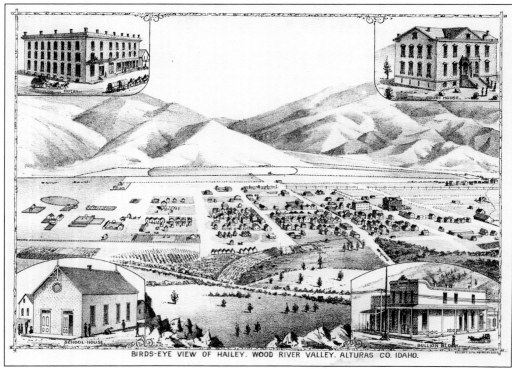

The town of Hailey appears in this illustration from *History of Idaho Territory* with Croy Canyon in the background. The insets show, clockwise from top left, the Alturas Hotel, Alturas County Courthouse, Bullion Block, and Hailey School.

In 1879, John Hailey, shown here with his family, filed a homestead claim for the townsite of Hailey, which was expanded to 440 acres and sold in 1882 to the Idaho & Oregon Land Development Company, owned by investors affiliated with the Union Pacific Railroad. John Hailey later served in Idaho's Territorial Congress and worked for the Idaho State Historical Society in the early 1900s.

In May 1881, T.E. Picote began the *Wood River Times*, the first daily paper published in Idaho. Valley towns competed with each other, supported by their newspapers, and this outspoken editor strongly promoted Hailey.

The author's great-grandparents, Matt and Isabelle Campbell McFall, moved to Bellevue, Idaho, in the spring of 1881 from the mining community of Eureka, Nevada. They built a boardinghouse in Broadford and the International Hotel in Bellevue in 1882. Here they are with their children (from left to right) John, Ella, and Stella around 1888. The author's grandmother, born in 1890, is not in the picture. (Author's photograph.)

The International Hotel, built by Matt McFall in 1882, was at the corner of Bellevue's Main and Oak Streets. According to Clark C. Spence's *For Wood River or Bust*, it was "one of the best in the Territory . . . Bellevue's best," and the center of town until it burned down in 1909.

Fish and game were plentiful in the Wood River Valley in the 1880s. Fishing and hunting were both forms of recreation and ways to obtain food. Showing how productive the fishery was, these trout were caught in one hour.

Hunters show off the pelts of coyotes, wolves, and cougars or bobcats they killed—"a good catch."

Skiing was a means of transportation and recreation in the valley's early days, done with homemade skis and one pole.

Valley residents are enjoying ice skating on Trail Creek, a popular and free form of recreation.

Guyer Hot Springs Resort was opened in 1882 by I.I. Lewis and Raymond Guyer on Warm Springs Creek just beyond the present Warm Springs Village. It became a popular social and health facility promoted by the railroads as "one of the greatest natural healing wonders and health resorts of the world," that could cure "rheumatism and kindred ailments."

THE GUYER HOT SPRINGS. I.I. LEWIS. MANAGER. 2 MILES WEST OF KETCHUM. ALTURAS CO. IDAHO.

Guyer Hot Springs Resort and its grounds are seen in this illustration from *History of Idaho Territory*. Its natural hot mineral waters attracted valley residents and tourists from 1882 until the 1920s.

Isabelle Campbell McFall's family followed her to Bellevue. Her brother Neil Campbell had the town's first blacksmith shop and operated a stagecoach line from Bellevue to the mining town of Muldoon, and the family owned 41 silver mines. This photograph shows Campbell Livery Stable on Main Street, across Oak Street from the International Hotel, with Neil and sons (from left to right) Stewart, George and Dan. The jitney's sign reads "International Hotel, Neil Campbell Livery."

The Bellevue Triangle, south of town, was settled early in the valley's history because of its good water and soil. Its farms supplied much of the valley's food. In 1884, the Brown & Milner Ditch was dug to bring 10,000 inches of Big Wood water from near Hailey to Bellevue and land south of town.

Three

THE OREGON SHORT LINE RAILROAD ARRIVES IN 1883

Even before the transcontinental railroad was completed in 1869, the Union Pacific wanted a route to the Northwest. In 1874, financier Jay Gould gained control of the Union Pacific with plans to access new markets—copper mines in Montana, Oregon's Willamette Valley, and the growing trade with East Asia.

In 1877, Gould hired newspaperman Robert E. Strahorn to tour the Northwest, publicize its economic potential, and help locate the best route for the new line. In 1881, Strahorn wrote *Resources and Attractions of Idaho Territory*, which praised the Wood River Valley and convinced the Union Pacific to build a branch line there.

In 1881, concerned that the Northern Pacific, then being built to Puget Sound, would have a monopoly over Northwest trade, the Union Pacific decided to build its own connection to Portland by the shortest route, using a subsidiary, the Oregon Short Line (OSL). Between May 1881 and November 1884, a new line was built from the Union Pacific's main line at Granger, Wyoming, through Idaho's Snake River basin, connecting at Huntington, Oregon, to a line being built east from Portland by Henry Villard's Oregon Railroad & Navigation Company.

After the route for a 69.4-mile line from Shoshone to Hailey was surveyed in 1882, Strahorn and others associated with the Union Pacific incorporated the Idaho & Oregon Land Improvement Company to acquire land for development in advance of the arrival of tracks. The company bought the townsites of Shoshone and Hailey, knowing that a branch line would be built connecting the towns to service the valley's booming silver industry. Hailey would be the line's terminus, and Strahorn's company intended to make it the industrial center of the valley.

The Wood River Branch reached Hailey in May 1883. The Philadelphia Smelter was the railroad's largest customer but was located north of Ketchum and had to send processed ore by wagon to Hailey for shipment. The smelter convinced the railroad to extend the rail line to its site, a decision opposed by Strahorn's forces, and it reached the smelter in August 1884. Shoshone, the junction where the branch joined the main OSL tracks, thrived as a railroad center through which all the valley's traffic passed.

The railroad transformed the Wood River Valley and provided a huge economic boost. Goods and passengers could flow in and out of the valley rapidly and cheaply. As Clark C. Spence wrote, "Wood River passed from lusty infancy to a more orderly adolescence." It brought an era of zation to the mining industry, as "Concentrating mills, smelters, tunneling, timbering, ...g, ventilating, and ore hauling all required capital beyond the means of most individuals," a year-round paid labor force was necessary.

Between 1883 and 1885, outside investors bought valley mines, bringing in new technology to expand their operations. The Mayflower Mine, acquired for $25,000, sold one year later to Chicago investors for $375,000. I.I. Lewis bought the Elkhorn Mine for $12,000 and refused an offer of $60,000. It produced nearly $185,000 in 1883. In 1884, English investors bought the Minnie Moore for $500,000, the Bullion for $1.05 million, and the Idahoan for $400,000. Owners of the Triumph Mine on the East Fork of the Wood River declined an offer of $40,000, and it later produced $20 million. In 1881, Wood River mines produced more than $1 million; in 1882, $2.5 million; in 1883, $3.5 million; in 1884, $5 million; with production rising to $9.245 million in 1887.

By 1883, Hailey had a municipal electrical system, and by November, a telephone line connected valley towns. By 1884, Ketchum was thriving, with 13 saloons, 4 restaurants, 2 hotels, 3 blacksmith shops, a brewery, and several stables. Bellevue had two newspapers, Hailey had three, and Ketchum had the *Ketchum Keystone*. By 1885, Hailey had 18 saloons and 12 gambling licenses. I.I. Lewis expanded his mining holdings, organized the First National Bank of Ketchum with $50,000 of capital, acquired the *Ketchum Keystone*, and erected buildings on Main Street.

The 1884 *Idaho Territorial Report* said that Wood River and Alturas County "is now . . . the richest silver-lead producing country in the world." The June 17, 1885, *Wood River Times* reported, "No other region on the face of the globe affords such a diversity and wealth of mineral formation as this."

Robert E. Strahorn
RAILROAD BUILDER

Mrs. Robert E. Strahorn
AUTHOR OF
"FIFTEEN THOUSAND MILES BY STAGE"

In 1877, Union Pacific financier Jay Gould hired journalist Robert Strahorn to tour the area to be served by a proposed Union Pacific line to the Northwest, publicize its potential, and help locate the best route. In 1882, Strahorn and other Union Pacific insiders formed the Idaho & Oregon Land Improvement Company to purchase land for development where the railroad planned to build depots. Strahorn convinced the Union Pacific to build a branch line into the Wood River Valley, and his company bought the townsite of Shoshone and, in June 1882, the Hailey townsite and surrounding land for $100,000, including the Croy and Quigley homesteads, intending to make Hailey the branch's terminus and the valley's commercial center. The company developed the railroad towns of Shoshone, Hailey, Mountain Home, Caldwell, Ontario, Payette, and New Weiser. Strahorn's wife, Carrie Adell, wrote travel articles for women's magazines. In 1911, they were published as *Fifteen Thousand Miles by Stage*, which became a best-seller. (Courtesy Zentmeyer family.)

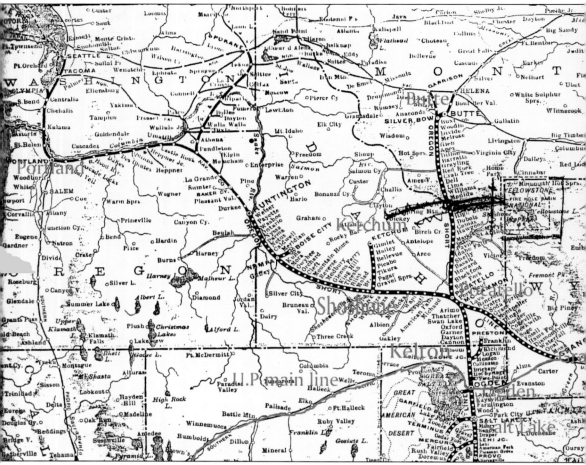

This map, from an 1898 Oregon Short Line schedule, shows several rail lines. First, Oregon Short Line tracks leave the main Union Pacific line at Granger, Wyoming, then go through Idaho to Portland, Oregon. The Wood River Branch from Shoshone to Ketchum is at center. Second, another Union Pacific subsidiary (the Utah & Northern Railroad) went north from Ogden, Utah, to Butte, Montana. Third, the main Union Pacific line from Omaha, Nebraska, to Sacramento, California, finished in 1869, goes southwest from Kelton, Utah. Wood River Valley passengers could ride the train to Shoshone and connect to trains going anywhere in the country.

In 1882–1883, the Kilpatrick brothers built the 69.4-mile Wood River Branch from Shoshone to Hailey using 3,000 men and 300 mules. They started at Picabo and worked in both directions. Since land between Picabo and Gannett was swampy, they had to bundle willow branches with rope and place them down with rocks and dirt on top to make the roadbed secure. (Courtesy Idaho State Historical Society.)

The Kilpatrick brothers homesteaded land around Picabo near Silver Creek, where this depot was located, and opened the Picabo General Store. Their grandson Bud Purdy was a friend of Ernest Hemingway, who used to hunt on the family's land on Silver Creek after 1939.

Shoshone was the junction between the Oregon Short Line's main line and the Wood River Branch. Shoshone thrived as a railroad town and was the de facto beginning of the valley, since all passengers and freight went through there. (Courtesy Idaho State Historical Society.)

Bellevue's first depot was a boxcar. This was the permanent Bellevue depot at the south end of town. A telegraph line arrived with the railroad, providing another connection to the outside world. Each depot had a telegraph office, and the Bellevue depot had two operators. (Courtesy Union Pacific Museum.)

Hailey was the intended terminus of the Wood River Branch when it arrived in May 1883. Hailey's permanent depot was finished in October 1886, and it had a second story where the depot agent lived and a first-floor office for a Western Union telegrapher.

— BY THE —

COMPLETION

— OF THE —

Oregon Short Line!

— Giving an —

ALL RAIL ROUTE

— To and from —

Wood River!

— THE —

UNION PACIFIC

Continues the shortest, quickest, best and

ONLY THROUGH RAIL ROUTE!

CLOSE CONNECTIONS AT

Shoshone, Pocatello and Ogden,

— For all Points —

NORTH, SOUTH, EAST AND WEST.
THROUGH TICKETS

— To —

OGDEN, SALT LAKE CITY

— And —

All Eastern Points,

— FOR SALE AT —

PACIFIC EXPRESS OFFICES

— AT —

HAILEY AND SHOSHONE.

Passenger and freight rates will always be as low as the lowest by this route.
For further information relative to freight or passenger rates call upon our address,
J. W. MORSE,
General Passenger Agent, U. P. R. R.
Omaha, Nebraska, or
P. H. McCONNELL,
General Agent U. P. R. R.
Salt Lake City.

The railroad transformed the Wood River Valley, making it possible for residents to travel anywhere in the country. It provided an economic boost, lowered the cost of transporting goods by $20 a ton, brought in outside investors who expanded the valley's mines and introduced industrial mining, and caused its cities to grow and mature.

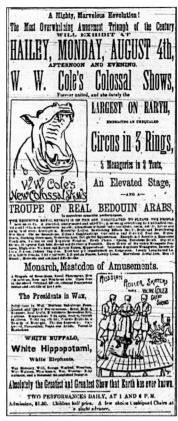

The train brought in outside influences, including a circus in 1884 with a variety of African animals and a "Troupe of Real Bedouin Arabs." Samson the elephant escaped and ran loose through Hailey, chased by gun-packing men shooting at him. The *Wood River Times* said elephant hunting was a popular sport and "Sampson seemed to enjoy the fun."

When the OSL extended its tracks to Ketchum in August 1884, the smelter gave the railroad land for its tracks and depot north of the town boundary in the Warm Springs area. The depot was east of the Big Wood River, near where the YMCA is located today.

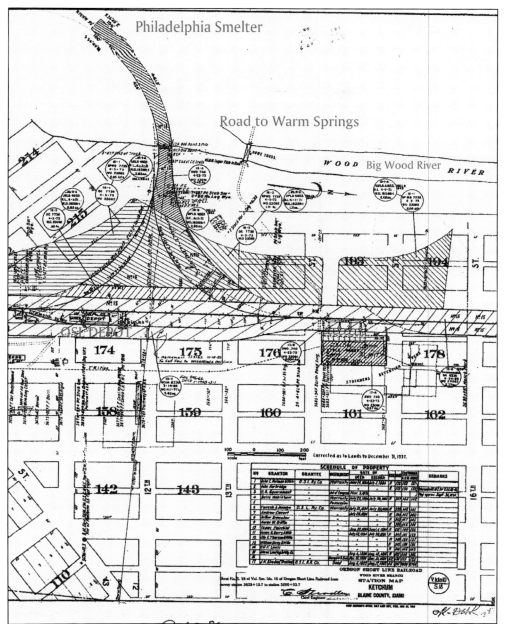

The Philadelphia Smelter Company was the Oregon Short Line's largest customer, but when the tracks stopped at Hailey, it had to send processed ore there by wagon for shipment. In 1884, the railroad was convinced to extend its tracks to the smelter, located on a bench north of Ketchum at the head of Warm Springs Canyon that had been expanded to 400 acres. The company also owned 1,000 acres west of the river. This map from the railroad survey shows the OSL depot on the east side of the river and the separate railroad bridge to take trains directly into the smelter via a wye. Trains coming north went into the smelter on the railroad bridge. When freight was unloaded and bullion loaded, trains backed up over the river on the other track and could then head south.

Every town had an opera house or hall. This is Ketchum's Fitzsimmons Metropolitan Hall, on Main Street looking south from Third Avenue beside the US Post Office/stationery store, around 1885. A grand celebration ball was held at the hall in August 1884 when the Oregon Short Line tracks arrived at Ketchum; music was provided by Prof. George Delius's Orchestra. (Photograph by Eugene Antz.)

The Wood River Valley received heavy snowfalls, creating problems for trains. The branch gained fame in 1887 when the first rotary snowplow in the West, and possibly the nation, cleared out the line in a successful test that led to the purchase of additional rotaries.

An Oregon Short Line train travels between Shoshone and the Wood River Valley, providing a connection with the outside world. (Photograph by Eugene Antz.)

This view of Bellevue looks west toward the Big Wood River in the early 1880s. By the fall of 1882, Bellevue had a daily newspaper, nine saloons, four churches, three blacksmiths, three hotels, seven attorneys, four physicians, three assayers, a wide variety of merchants, and "the best race track in the northwest," according to the *Bellevue Chronicle*.

This view of Ketchum in 1885 looks north toward Warm Springs Canyon and Griffin Butte. (Photograph by Eugene Antz.)

From left to right, Bert Griffith, Charlie Venable, and Oscar Griffith stand on Ketchum's Main Street looking north toward Griffin Butte. The Comstock & Clark General Store is on the far right at what became Sun Valley Road. (Courtesy Mary Jane Griffith family.)

In 1884, I.I. Lewis constructed two brick buildings on Ketchum's Main Street. This is the Pinkham/Lewis building on the west side of Main Street at Second Street, housing the Lewis-Lemon General Store. It later become Greenhow & Rumsey Mercantile, the Ketchum Post Office in the late 1890s, the Griffith Grocery in the 1920s, and most recently the Cornerstone Restaurant. It is the new site for the Ketchum Culinary Institute.

This is the second brick building constructed by I.I. Lewis in 1884, the First National Bank of Ketchum on the east side of Main and Second Streets. Lewis and his son George stand in front. The building is now Rocky Mountain Hardware.

45

Isaac's son Horace Lewis stands in front of the First National Bank of Ketchum, which was organized by the Lewis family with $50,000 of capital. Horace and his brother George worked at the bank.

This is Horace and Kate Lewis's house with a stagecoach in front. The house is now Elephant's Perch at Sun Valley Road and East Street.

The Baxter Hotel was on Ketchum's Main Street south of Lewis's First National Bank. Free baths (hot and cold) were available to guests. Like many large wooden buildings that were heated by wood or coal, the Baxter Hotel burned down. This advertisement is from the July 9, 1893, *Ketchum Keystone*.

PAUL P. BAXTE
KE
THE OLDEST H___ ON WOOD RIVER.

The Dining-room the Largest in the State.

A First-Class Metropolitan House.

Good Beds and Furniture Throughout the House.
FINE SYSTEM OF WATER-WORKS.

Twenty-Five New Rooms---Large, Airy and Well Furnished.
Comfortable Parlors and Reading Rooms.

FREE BATHS
Hot and Cold, for the accommodation of guests.

FREE 'BUS TO AND FROM RAILROAD DEPOT.

The Location Central and Convenient to the Business Houses,
Postoffice, Bank, Etc.

Go to the BAXTER HOTEL.
TERMS MODERATE.

The Comstock & Clark building was built in 1887 as a general store in Ketchum. In 1920, Jack Lane bought the building for Lane Mercantile to sell provisions to sheep ranchers. It was a hangout for Union Pacific managers when Sun Valley was built in 1936. It is now the Enoteca Restaurant, located at Main Street and Sun Valley Road.

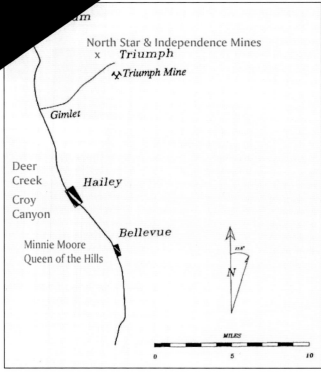

North Star & Independence Mines
x **Triumph**

✗ Triumph Mine

Gimlet

Deer
Creek

Hailey

Croy
Canyon

Bellevue

Minnie Moore
Queen of the Hills

N

MILES

0   5   10

The Minnie Moore and Queen of the Hills in Galena Gulch, west of Bellevue, were two of the Valley's most productive mines, producing $10 to $15 million in ore. The Nay Nay and Walla Walla Mines were on Deer Creek, north of Hailey. The Triumph and North Star Mines were on the East Fork of the Big Wood, and the Independence Mine was in Elkhorn's Independence Gulch. This map is from *Historic Mines of Blaine County, Idaho.*

This drawing shows the underground workings at the Nay Nay Mine on Deer Creek, illustrating how industrial mining changed mining techniques, requiring extensive capital provided by outside investors. (Courtesy Evelyn Phillips.)

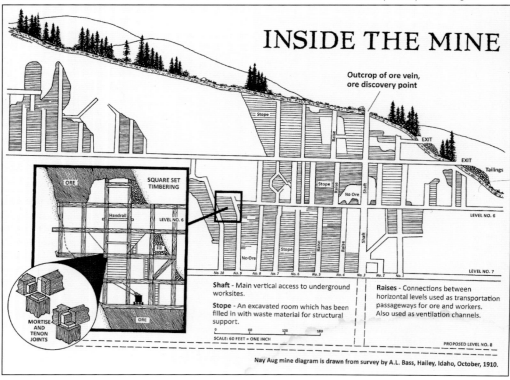

INSIDE THE MINE

Outcrop of ore vein,
ore discovery point

Stope

Raise

EXIT

EXIT

Tailings

ORE

SQUARE SET
TIMBERING

Handrail

LEVEL NO. 6

Fill

No Ore

ORE

MORTISE
AND
TENON
JOINTS

Stope

Raise

No Ore

Shaft

LEVEL NO. 6

Stope

Raise

Raise

Shaft

LEVEL NO. 7

No. 10   No. 5   No. 8   No. 7   No. 6   No. 5   No. 4   No. 3   No. 2   No. 1

Shaft - Main vertical access to underground worksites.

Stope - An excavated room which has been filled in with waste material for structural support.

SCALE: 60 FEET = ONE INCH
0   60   120   180

Raises - Connections between horizontal levels used as transportation passageways for ore and workers. Also used as ventilation channels.

PROPOSED LEVEL NO. 8

Nay Aug mine diagram is drawn from survey by A.L. Bass, Hailey, Idaho, October, 1910.

Concentrating mills known as stamp mills, such as this one at Walla Walla Mine on Deer Creek, used heavy steel stamps or pestles to pound ore and crush it into powder to make it easier and cheaper to transport to smelters for processing. Water wheels that powered the mill can be seen on the left. Such formal portraits of workers and their families were popular.

The Philadelphia Smelter Company purchased the North Star Mine in 1883 for $30,000, and in 1887, built a modern 10-stamp mill for $15,000, shown here behind a Ketchum Fast Freight wagon loaded with timber. The company reported it sold the mine in 1916 for $60,000 after it produced $600,000 of ore, although Victoria Mitchell's report on the mine said the price was $150,000, with $29,000 paid in 1916.

The Independence Mine was one mile north of the Triumph Mine, in Elkhorn's Independence Gulch. The mine's entry is up the hill, the tailings pile is the white area in the middle, and the stamp mill is at the bottom. Ore was sent downhill to the mill, where it was crushed by heavy stamps.

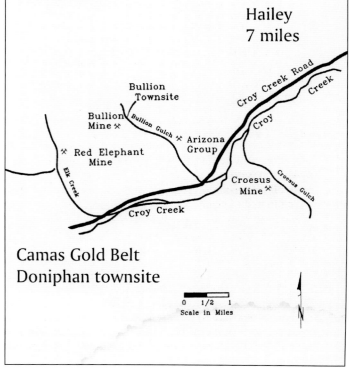

This map from *Historic Mines of Blaine County* shows some of the primary mines in Croy Canyon. Camas Gold Belt mines and the town of Doniphan were farther west in Croy Canyon. Gilman Village was at the head of Bullion Canyon, and the Bullion townsite was up the gulch, where several major mines were located.

The narrow Bullion Canyon, seven miles west of Hailey, contained the Mayflower, Bullion, Jay Gould, and Ophir Mines, which were connected by tunnels, and the Red Elephant, which was not connected. The mines employed 500 men, and 700 people lived in the Bullion townsite, described by Clark C. Spence as "2 miles long and 18 inches wide." The mines produced $2.7 million in ore by 1887.

"BULLION MINE", BULLION, ALTURAS CO. IDAHO. PROPERTY OF THE WOOD RIVER GOLD & SILVER MINING CO.

"MAY FLOWER MINE", BULLION, IDAHO, MAY FLOWER CONSOLIDATED SILVER MINING CO. OF CHICAGO.

This drawing from *History of Idaho Territory* shows the Bullion Mine (left) and Mayflower Mine in Bullion Gulch off of Croy Canyon.

Blacksmithing was a critical skill for the mining industry. Strain on freight wagons "made a blacksmith shop in the diggings imperative," according to the 75th Anniversary Edition of the *Hailey Times* in 1956. "Practically everything used in or around the mine passed through the blacksmith's forge." Pictured here are blacksmiths at the Homestake Mine in Deadwood, Dakota Territory, in the early 1880s. Andrew Lundin, the author's great-grandfather, holds a hammer, indicating he was head blacksmith. (Author's photograph.)

These marchers supported the Broadford union miners who struck in the winter of 1885, opposing an attempt by mine owners to reduce wages from $3.50 a day to $3. Idaho's governor threatened to bring in troops, the strike ended without significant violence, and wages were reduced. Major strikes occurred in silver mines in Coeur d'Alene in 1892 and 1898–1899 involving violent confrontations between labor and management.

Four

Philadelphia Smelter
Becomes Economic Force

In anticipation of the arrival of the railroad in 1883, the Philadelphia Smelter set out to "control the entire Wood River country and furnish a profitable market to the whole mineral region surrounding in Idaho and adjoining territories" in order to "compete with the world," according to Clark C. Spence.

The smelter expanded significantly and purchased 14 mines: the Muldoon Group in the Little Wood River basin (for $100,000), the North Star Group ($30,000) and the Paymaster Group on the East Fork of the Big Wood, the Silver Star Group of 11 mines ($50,000) in the Little Smoky Mining District over the Dollarhide Summit, and mines in the Warm Springs Mining District and along the Big Lost River. The company spent $75,000 to build a smelter and tram at Muldoon, and concentrating mills were built at the North Star and Silver Star Mines.

The smelter's site was expanded to 400 acres, and two new buildings and a second smokestack were built. An ore house 200 feet by 50 feet was built where ore was prepared for the furnaces. A road along its side was wide enough for two loaded wagons to pass each other. The second building was a 60-foot-by-60-foot furnace house with two new state-of-the-art 50-ton furnaces, expanding the smelter's capacity to 180 tons a day. Power was provided by two 40-horsepower water wheels driven by water from Warm Springs Creek, brought to the site by a ditch from Guyer Hot Springs. In 1887, the ditch was replaced by an elevated V-shaped flume that carried 400 inches of hot water. The smelter had 20 kilns that could convert wood to 60,000 bushels of charcoal per month.

The expanded smelter began operations in August 1883, processing ore from 52 mines throughout the entire region. It reduced from 80 to 130 tons of ore a day that averaged 50 percent lead and 100 ounces of silver per ton, producing 40 to 60 tons of base bullion, enough to fill three railcars. In September 1883, the smelter shipped 57 carloads of bullion. By the end of 1883, the smelter had produced 300,000 tons of bullion, worth $3 million.

The Philadelphia Smelter became the largest industrial enterprise in Idaho Territory, "the most complete smelting works in the West," according to Spence, making Ketchum "the most healthy mining town on Wood River." The smelter used the most advanced methods and equipment and become the valley's dominant economic power and largest employer. After 1883, the valley's four smaller smelters could not compete and went out of business. In 1884, according to Spence, the valley was the "most progressive region in the region." By 1885, between 250 and 300 men worked in the smelter and its mines.

In 1884, Horace Lewis organized the Ketchum & Challis Toll Road Company to build a toll road over Trail Creek Summit to reach mines around Challis. Ore wagons drawn by 20-mule teams carried up to 18,000 pounds and took two weeks to make the 160-mile round-trip between Ketchum and Challis, averaging 12–16 miles a day. Lewis also owned a stagecoach company that carried passengers and mail to and from Challis, Clayton, Bayhorse, Custer, and Bonanza and another that served areas along the Salmon River. Ketchum Fast Freight operated out of a large facility across the Big Wood River from the Philadelphia Smelter and used 30 sets of wagons and 700 horses in its operations.

In 1883, the Philadelphia Smelter was rebuilt and expanded to 400 acres. One new building had two 50-ton Colorado furnaces (to supplement its existing two 40-ton furnaces), rock breakers, sampling works, and a 50-foot smokestack. It became, according to Clark C. Spence, the "most complete smelting works in the West," with "all the machinery for a complete first class plant" designed to "compete with the world."

Silver bullion was kept in this small building, surrounded by waste rock produced during smelting. In 1883, seven wagons brought 50 tons of ore a day to the smelter from valley mines. Powered by water from Warm Springs Creek, the smelter processed an average of 80 to 130 tons of ore daily, producing 40 to 60 tons of base bullion. By the end of 1883, the smelter produced 300,000 tons of silver bullion, worth $3 million.

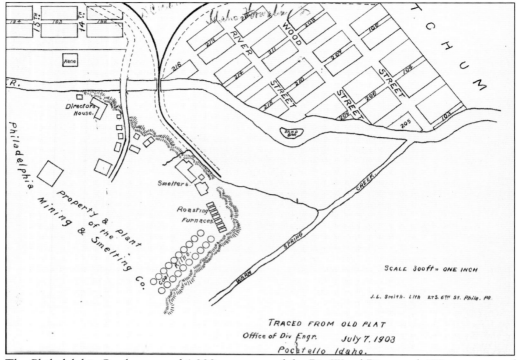

The Philadelphia Smelter owned 1,000 acres east of the Big Wood River and 400 acres west of the river, which was annexed by Ketchum in 1884 as the Rhodes Addition. This part of the plat map shows the smelter site and the two bridges over the river, one for wagons and the other for the railroad. Land east of the river was platted into streets and blocks but was not developed.

Railroad tracks went over the Big Wood River directly into the Philadelphia Smelter by a separate bridge south of the wagon bridge. It is not clear why the man is sitting on the tracks. (Photograph by Eugene Antz.)

In 1882, the Philadelphia Smelter Company bought the mines at Muldoon in the Little Wood River Valley for $100,000 and spent $75,000 to build a smelter that produced $200,000 of silver, some seen here waiting for shipment. The mines played out, and in 1885, the company moved the mining equipment to its North Star Mine.

In 1883, the Philadelphia Smelter Company purchased the Silver Star Group of mines in the Little Smoky Mining District for $50,000. Ore was brought over the Dollarhide Summit to Ketchum for processing. The company spent $76,000 building a 20-stamp mill in the fall of 1887 that operated one month before closing because of the silver depression. A 1948 publication said $500,000 was spent on the mine. Here, Bellevue mining historian Tom Blanchard stands by the Silver Star mill in 2016. (Author's photograph.)

Horace Lewis's Ketchum Fast Freight forwarding house/express office and a loaded ore wagon are in the foreground, and the Philadelphia Smelter is behind at the head of Warm Springs Canyon. Freight wagons brought ore to the smelter from 52 mines in the Wood River Valley and Smoky Mining Districts over the Dollarhide Summit, Sawtooth Valley over the Galena Summit, and around Challis over the Trail Creek Summit.

A Ketchum Fast Freight wagon stands in front of the company's headquarters. The company used 30 sets of wagons and 700 horses and had a through-freight tariff arrangement with the Oregon Short Line, so one fee was charged to transport goods from their origin to their ultimate destination.

A Ketchum Fast Freight wagon at the Clayton Mine near Challis is ready to start the trip over the Galena Summit to Ketchum. Horace Lewis also owned a stagecoach company that carried goods and mail to mining communities around Challis and another that served areas along the Salmon River.

A tollhouse was located at the top of Trail Creek Summit on the Ketchum-Challis Toll Road, built by Horace Lewis in 1884.

Ketchum Fast Freight wagons were hauled by 20-mule teams, carried up to 18,000 pounds of ore, and took two weeks to complete the round-trip from Challis to Ketchum, averaging 12–16 miles a day. Wagons stopped overnight at camps established by Lewis.

Around 1885, a Ketchum Fast Freight wagon climbs the Ketchum-Challis Toll Road over the Trail Creek Summit, which had a 12 percent grade, hairpin turns, and dangerous curves. The road has been rebuilt and straightened and now has a seven percent grade, but it is still listed on dangerousroads.org, where it is described as "not for the faint of heart." (Photograph by Eugene Antz.)

Five

AGRICULTURE BECOMES THE VALLEY'S ECONOMIC BASE

As Clark C. Spence writes in *For Wood River or Bust*, "For mining communities . . . there is a time to be born and a time to die." The 1880s were the height of the Wood River Valley's mining era, when the production of its mines was phenomenal, yielding more than $14 million in silver and nearly $5 million in lead, the bulk of it before 1890: "silver-lead ores dictated both the rise and decline of such centers as Bellevue, Hailey, Bullion, Broadford, Ketchum, and Muldoon."

Showing how closely this remote area was linked to the outside world, the valley's mining boom came to a sudden end in 1888 as the international silver depression devastated the national economy, the result of several decades of federal gold and silver coinage policies. Silver prices tumbled in 1888 and fell further in 1892. On May 5, 1893, a Wall Street panic known as "Industrial Black Friday" caused the price of silver to cave, ending the Gilded Age and creating a full-blown depression said to be worse than the Great Depression of the 1930s. By the end of 1893, more than 15,000 businesses and 642 banks closed, and 20 percent of American workers (between two and three million) had lost their jobs. The hard times lasted until the Klondike Gold Rush of 1898 ended the depression.

The depression hit the Wood River Valley hard. Its mines and smelters closed and inhabitants left, abandoning towns such as Bolton, Bullion, Gilman, Broadford, Gimlet, Doniphan, Hays, and Muldoon. Bellevue, Hailey, and Ketchum survived as centers of transportation and commerce. Between 1887 and 1890, Bellevue's population dropped from 3,000 to 892, Hailey's from 4,000 to 1,073, and Ketchum's from 2,000 to 465. Ketchum dropped to 300 by 1900. "The Wood River Mining Region is deader than a lime fossil," reported the *Ketchum Keystone* of October 12, 1893. The author's great-grandparents Matt and Isabelle McFall moved in 1893 to Shoshone, still a thriving railroad center, where they built the McFall Hotel.

Most railroads went into receivership in the 1890s, including the Union Pacific and the Oregon Short Line. In 1897, E.H. Harriman led a group that bought the Union Pacific and its subsidiaries out of bankruptcy and expanded them to control much of the rail transportation in the West, prospering as the West grew. The Harriman fortune made it possible for his son Averell to control the Union Pacific and build Sun Valley in 1936.

Central Idaho's economy changed to agriculture in the 1890s, and the railroad made the summer grazing of sheep in the valley possible. The *Salt Lake Tribune* reported that Idaho prospered in notwithstanding the depression in mining:

> [Idaho's] irrigating canals have been extended more and more; acres been brought under the plow, and . . . all it needs in Idaho is to utilize the water that flows by toward the sea upon the land to give to it life, to make one of the richest of States. It has no end of magnificent land—land that produces in abundance and of the best quality everything that grows in the Temperate Zone.

The National Reclamation Act of 1902 provided federal money for irrigation projects in the arid West, funding construction of dams on the Snake and Big Wood Rivers. Twin Falls was platted in 1904, and Milner Dam was completed in 1905 to irrigate the areas around the new town. The $5.8-million Minidoka project, completed in 1909, irrigated a large part of central Idaho with seven dams and 1,600 miles of canals. The $2-million Magic Dam on the Big Wood River was completed in 1910, and its four main canals irrigated 75,000 acres around Shoshone, including the new towns of Richfield, Gooding, and Dietrich. Irrigation made the desert bloom, attracting many immigrants. Idaho's population grew from 88,000 in 1890 to 161,000 in 1900, then 325,000 in 1910, and 431,000 by 1920. The Oregon Short Line offered special immigrant rates and boxcars to transport household goods, farming implements, and stock for $150. Shoshone prospered because of the new dams and irrigation projects being built around it and continued to be the economic hub for the Wood River Valley as its railroad junction.

World War I started in Europe in 1914, creating a demand for Idaho's agricultural products (grain, wool, and lamb) and minerals (lead, silver, and copper), which increased when the United States entered the war in 1917. Farmers borrowed heavily to expand their operations. The number of sheep in Idaho increased from 14,000 in the late 1860s to 614,000 in 1890, then to 2.65 million in 1918. Sheep kept valley towns busy in the summers, but they were nonexistent in the winter. When a new hotel and plunge were built at Guyer Hot Springs for $25,000 in 1914, the contractor said Ketchum was "just a whistling post, with about thirty or forty families living there."

Fred and Frank Gooding moved to the Wood River Valley in 1881. They cut wood for the Philadelphia Smelter and ties for the railroad and brought in some of the valley's first sheep. In 1888, they moved to a ranch that became the town of Gooding and were Idaho's largest sheep owners. Fred Gooding was Idaho's governor from 1905 to 1909 and a US senator from 1918 to 1928. (Courtesy Idaho State Historical Society.)

Sheep Grazing in the Sawtooth Mts. Idaho.

In 1887, the Goodings were the first to trail sheep through the Wood River Valley into the Stanley Basin (shown here) to spend the summer. The sheep returned through the valley in the fall to their winter homes in the desert. This began a tradition celebrated by the valley's Trailing of the Sheep Festival, held every October.

The economy's change from mining to sheep raising is illustrated by these sheep grazing around kilns that created charcoal for the abandoned Muldoon Smelter in the Little Wood Valley in the early 1900s. (Photograph by Martyn Mallory.)

James Laidlaw was a Scottish immigrant who helped start the region's sheep industry. Here, Laidlaw (right) and a shepherd stand in front of abandoned kilns at the Muldoon Smelter. Laidlaw bred Panama sheep suitable for Idaho—hearty, strong, and able to produce bigger lambs on scant rangeland. His ranch is now part of Flattop Ranch in the Little Wood Basin.

After the Kilpatrick brothers built the branch line from Shoshone to Hailey, they homesteaded land around Picabo and established one of the area's early sheep ranches, shown here.

Wagons used by shepherds were early versions of a camper, containing a bed, stove, storage, and space for their needs for several months. Wagons were hauled from site to site by horses as sheep moved between grazing areas. A shepherd's life was a lonely one, spending summers alone in the mountains with only sheep and dogs for company.

Basques were hired to tend valley sheep. They often carved arborglyphs (pictures and words) on aspen trees that still can be seen. Many Basques took sheep for their pay, eventually starting their own ranches. Basque culture is an important part of Idaho's history celebrated by many events, including the valley's Trailing of the Sheep festival. Many shepherds are now Peruvians.

These sheep wait to be shipped by train at the Ketchum depot in the 700-acre Ketchum Livestock Association's stockyards, which were purchased from the Philadelphia Company Trust in 1903. Smoke from a train can be seen in the background. The stockyards have been developed into residential neighborhoods.

Chutes were used to load sheep onto train cars. In the 1920s, there were between one and two million sheep in the region. Ketchum and Hill City on Camas Prairie shipped more sheep than anywhere in the country and were second only to Sydney, Australia.

Sheep loaded onto a boxcar at Ketchum wait to be taken to markets outside the Wood River Valley.

Education was important to early settlers, and valley towns built permanent structures for their children. The Ketchum School, shown here, was built in 1887.

Children often used skis to get to school because of the valley's heavy snowfalls. Ketchum's schoolhouse can be seen in the background.

In 1888, Robert Strahorn bought Hailey Hot Springs in Croy Canyon (shown here in the early 1890s). He spared no expense to make the resort a high-end tourist attraction. A travel publication said its waters were good to treat neuralgia, paralysis, dyspepsia, and inflammatory or mercurial rheumatism. The hotel burned down in 1899.

Union Pacific financier Jay Gould, who was responsible for building the Oregon Short Line to Portland, visited the valley several times in the 1890s. In July 1891, Gould came to the valley by private train with a locomotive, tender, baggage car, commissary car, and two private drawing coaches. His party included private secretaries, cooks, porters, and other attendants.

This view of Ketchum in 1900 looks east toward Trail Creek and the Pioneer Mountains. The road on the right became Sun Valley Road after Sun Valley was developed in 1936.

I.I. Lewis, shown here in 1901, was one of Ketchum's founders and a successful businessman, worth over $92,000 (nearly $2.4 million today).

The Lewis family is shown camping with horses and carriages at Alturas Lake north of Ketchum over the Galena Summit, a popular activity for valley residents.

Wood River Valley residents adopted new technology when it became available. Here, a family used a car instead of horses to go camping in the early 1900s. (Photograph by Martyn Mallory.)

A family car is parked in front of Isaac Lewis's house in Ketchum in the early 1900s.

People watch the 1903 Fourth of July parade on Bellevue's Main Street from the street and on the balcony of Matt McFall's International Hotel. Neil Campbell's blacksmith shop and livery stable are beyond the hotel south of Oak Street. The cart is ridden by Rodney Reed, who became an Idaho state senator. One of the valley's first automobiles is in the parade.

The mining industry also adopted technological advances. Here, a steam engine hauls ore carts, replacing donkeys and oxen.

I.E. Rockwell and Althea Venable pose at Rockwell's home in Bellevue. In 1900, Rockwell bought the Minnie Moore Mine for $30,000, reopening one of the valley's historic mines. It was operated off and on through the 1970s. Rockwell later represented the valley in the state legislature and owned one of Ketchum's livery stables.

Minnie Moore's Hoist Room (shown here in 1902) contained equipment to raise and lower miners into the mineshaft. Veins being worked could be thousands of feet below the surface, often below the water level, so massive pumps were required to keep mines clear of water. In 1903, a fire in the hoist room trapped five miners underground, but they were rescued.

In 1908, I.E. Rockwell's Idaho Consolidated Mines Company built a new mill that could process 250 tons of ore a day from the Minnie Moore, Relief, and Queen of the Hills Mines. It was powered by a hydroelectric plant on the Big Wood River that used Westinghouse generators. Canals were dug to supply water to operate the machinery.

The bunkhouse at the North Star Mine was destroyed by an avalanche on February 25, 1917, killing 11 men and injuring more. The company settled lawsuits over the incident for $55,000. Trees were cut down in the gulches along the valley's rivers to provide wood for the mining industry and housing, leaving steep slopes that were prone to slides.

Guyer Hot Springs Resort was not just a summer resort. Here, a family enjoys skiing there in the late 1890s.

In 1914, a new hotel and plunge were built for $25,000 at Guyer Hot Springs. It was a grand two-story gabled structure with 18 rooms, a spacious dance floor, and lawn tennis. The resort was promoted as a vacation spa and a health resort and was Ketchum's social hub. Its opening dress ball was a "veritable Midsummer Night's Dream," according to the *Hailey Times*, where costumed guests danced until 4:30 a.m.

In 1900, the author's great-grandparents built the McFall Hotel in Shoshone, a thriving railroad junction profiting from Reclamation Act projects built around it and called the center of "The Best Dam County" in the nation. The author's grandmother Alberta McFall appears in the picture. Ernest Hemingway was known to stop at the hotel for a drink on his way to Ketchum. (Author's photograph.)

The Reclamation Act of 1902 provided federal funds to build irrigation projects in arid Western states. Central Idaho benefitted greatly as dams were built on the Snake and Big Wood Rivers that irrigated vast tracts of desert land, making the desert bloom. Magic Dam, its reservoir, and irrigation canals (shown here in 1908) were completed on the Big Wood River in 1910 at a cost of $2 million. It was said to be the highest earthen dam in the world at the time. The system's water went through four main canals totaling 200 miles, irrigating 75,000 acres in five tracts around Shoshone: Richfield, North Gooding, North Shoshone, South Gooding, and Dietrich.

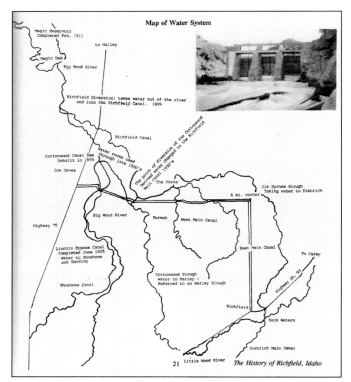

Map of Water System

The History of Richfield, Idaho

This map from *The History of Richfield, Idaho, "The Biggest Little Town in Idaho"* shows the distribution of water from Magic Dam to areas around Shoshone. Developers subdivided irrigated land, which was sold through land openings. Land sold for a few dollars an acre, while water rights cost $30 to $40 an acre or more. The Oregon Short Line offered special immigrant rates and boxcars to transport 20,000 pounds of goods and equipment to Idaho for $150.

The land opening for the Kilpatrick brothers' 4,000-acre farm near Picabo in 1917 offered land with water rights for $70 per acre. Picabo townsite lots were also for sale. (Courtesy Bud Purdy.)

LAND OPENING

— THE —

Kilpatrick Brothers' Farm

PICABO, BLAINE COUNTY, IDAHO

July 17, 1917

FOUR THOUSAND ACRES

of improved land, growing alfalfa, sugar beets, wheat, oats, barley, rye and all kinds of meadow grasses.

Water rights are first class in every particular. Excellent domestic water.

Not an acre sold until Opening Day. Will begin showing the land July 14. Subdivided in 40's, 80's and 160's.

$70 per acre, average price including independent water rights with every acre

$20 an acre cash, at time of purchase

Ten years time on balance, payments at straight 6 per cent per annum, interest payable once a year. Abstracts furnished all purchasers, showing the property clear of all incumbrances. Sales Office will open at 6 o'clock A. M. and close at 12 midnight. A general discount will be allowed on all purchases of land and town lots of 5 per cent for the one day only, July 17, 1917. Should you wish to pay cash for the property you purchase, an additional 5 per cent will be allowed on all cash purchases at all times.

TOWNSITE OPENING

Picabo, July 17, 1917

The opening sale of lots in Picabo Townsite will occur the same day as the land opening. Not a lot in the town has been sold. Great opportunities for Business Men.

Special Railway Rates in effect July 14 to July 20.

For Illustrated Literature, Address Land Office, Picabo, Idaho.

Six

KETCHUM BEFORE THE ARRIVAL OF SUN VALLEY

When World War I ended, demand for Idaho's agricultural products and minerals dropped, and prices collapsed. Farmers were unable to pay their loans, and banks failed all over the state. This resulted in an agricultural depression in the 1920s, well before the Great Depression. "The Roaring Twenties hit Idaho with a dull thud," said the *Idaho Statesman* Centennial Edition.

Western farming states were hit hard by the agricultural depression during a time when the rest of the country was booming. According to the Idaho State Historical Society's *Idaho's Agricultural Development, 1908–1929*,

> Agricultural prices collapsed everywhere in 1920–1921, and farm states like Idaho went through a decade of financial disaster and travail before their economic misfortunes grew into a great world depression after 1929. National efforts to solve agricultural marketing problems did not get very far during a period when other segments of the economy enjoyed a period of prosperity, but reclamation projects in Idaho continued to expand.

Irrigation projects brought some economic relief around Shoshone. These included the $4-million Big Wood Canal bypass in the 1920s; the American Falls Dam, built between 1925 and 1927 and taking water out of the Snake River at Milner to irrigate land around Shoshone; and the Milner-Shoshone Canal (also known as the Milner-Gooding Canal), built between 1928 and 1932 to bring water from American Falls to areas around Gooding and Shoshone. The Perrine Memorial Bridge at Twin Falls was completed in 1927.

Outside capital reopened some of the Wood River Valley's historic mines in the early 1900s, such as the Minnie Moore and Queen of the Hills Mines west of Bellevue, the Triumph and North Star Mines on East Fork, and a few others. However, the industry never reached its halcyon days of the 1880s. The valley was in a down cycle from the end of World War I into the 1930s.

Federal legislation provided a stimulus to the valley's silver industry in the 1930s. The 1929 stock market crash depressed the value of silver, which reached a low of 24¢ per ounce in December 1932. Silver interests, led by senators from Western silver mining states, began a campaign to convince the government to create demand for silver. In May 1934, the president recommended that Congress "increase the amount of silver in our monetary stocks with the ultimate objective of having and maintaining one-fourth of the monetary value in silver and three-fourths in gold."

The Silver Purchase Act of 1934 authorized the president to nationalize silver and required people to sell their silver to the US Mint. On April 10, 1935, the US Treasury announced the price of 71.11¢ per ounce for newly mined silver, raising the price two weeks later to 77.57¢, pushing the market price to 81¢ per ounce. The federal government bought all domestically mined silver at a premium over the world market price until 1964. One of the primary effects of the act was to help the silver mining interests in the United States, causing mines throughout the West to reopen, including several in the Wood River Valley. Critics of the law, such as Milton Friedman, said the silver purchase program was adopted in response to a small but politically potent group and gave silver producers a large short-term subsidy at the cost of any long-run monetary role for silver.

When Count Felix Schaffgotsch arrived in February 1936 looking for a site for Averell Harriman's ski resort, Ketchum was a small mountain village that was often snowbound in the winter, when only half of its 270 residents stayed in town. It was on a Union Pacific line, but trains from Shoshone only ran a few times a week if they could get through the deep snow that often closed the track. The summer's sheep industry was nonexistent. Griffith Grocery Store was open two hours a day. Ketchum Kamp was the town's largest saloon. Lane Mercantile was the town's general store and the meeting place for sheep men. The count stayed at Bald Mountain Hot Springs Lodge after it was dug out of the snow and got meals from a local woman, since the town's restaurants were closed. The count was impressed by the lodge's pool, which used natural hot water from Guyer Hot Springs, and wanted a similar pool for the new ski area. He was also impressed by the locals, who were capable skiers using primitive homemade equipment.

Sun Valley reinvented the Wood River Valley, changing it from an abandoned mining area supported by sheep herding into an international tourist destination for skiing and mountain recreation. Tourism has been the valley's economic base ever since.

Federal subsidies further encouraged the production of lead and zinc during World War II for the war effort, keeping production of the Triumph Mine at capacity throughout the war. In 1943, the Triumph Mine was one of the 10 top producing mines in Idaho for gold, silver, lead, and zinc, and in 1948 was the largest producer in southern Idaho. Between 1884 and 1967, the Triumph produced $39,719,400 worth of metals, the North Star produced $8,685,100 between 1883 and 1942, and the Independence produced $3,335,800 between 1884 and 1933.

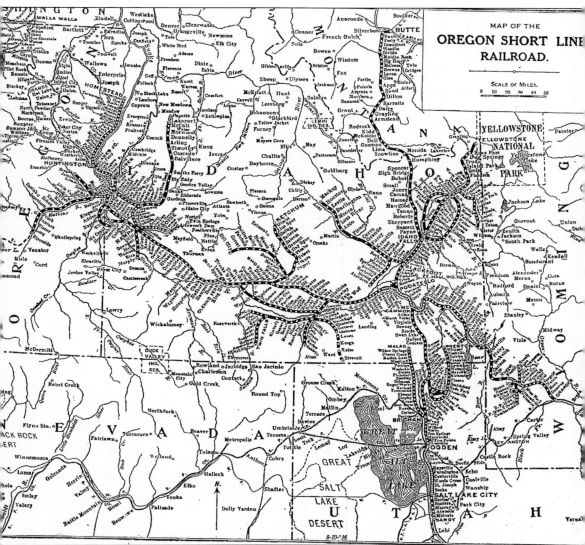

This map, from a 1916 Oregon Short Line schedule, shows its tracks leaving the main Union Pacific cross-country tracks at Granger, Wyoming, going into southeast Idaho to Pocatello, following the Snake River to Huntington, Oregon, and then along the Columbia River toward Portland. The Wood River Branch, seen at center, had 13 stops between Shoshone and Ketchum, most serving now-unknown farming communities: Marley, Richfield, Pageri, Tikura, Priest, Picabo, Hay Spur, Gannett, Balaam, Bellevue, Hailey, Zinc Spur, and Gimlet. The map shows the many branch lines into new farming towns built around areas irrigated by Reclamation Act projects. The Utah & Northern, going north from Salt Lake City through eastern Idaho to Butte, Montana, was then part of the Oregon Short Line.

Neil Campbell's son George was Blaine County sheriff in the 1920s and 1930s. Another son, Stewart (shown here), was Idaho's inspector of mines from 1920 to 1932, a powerful position. Stewart Campbell made significant changes to the position, enhanced its power and prestige, and wrote professional treatises about mining in the Wood River Valley. The Campbell family owned 41 silver mines over the years. (Courtesy Idaho State Historical Society.)

In 1923, the Minnie Moore Mine was reopened after being closed during the 1910s, and a headframe was built for the Allen Shaft (shown here in 1925) to access the mine. The Rockwell Shaft was drilled in the early 1930s, and exploration work continued after 1935.

The Minnie Moore headframe is in the foreground, and the Queen of the Hills Mine is in the background. Irwin Rockwell and Stewart Campbell combined forces and sought financing in a 1938 prospectus to find the infamous "lost vein of silver" below the Rockwell Fault, predicting great returns. Until 1971, the two mines were jointly operated by the Silver Star–Queens Company, formed by Stewart Campbell. (Courtesy Idaho State Historical Society.)

After the North Star Mine was purchased from the Philadelphia Smelter Company Trust in 1916, $314,000 was spent on development, including a new mill with a capacity of 150 tons per day (shown here in 1917), making it Blaine County's most productive mine that year. In 1920, the North Star and Independence Mines were connected by tunnel. In 1936, the Triumph and North Star Mines were connected by tunnel, and in 1940, the Triumph Mine Co. acquired the North Star.

In 1927, a new head frame was built at the Triumph Mine (shown here in the 1930s). During World War II, the federal government subsidized the recovery of lead and zinc for the war effort, keeping the mine's production at capacity throughout the war. Fire destroyed the Triumph mill in 1947, valued at $300,000, which was replaced by a 300-tons-per-day mill in 1951. Production was suspended in 1957, although exploration work continued through the 1980s. The Triumph has been a source of significant environmental issues over the years.

In 1930, a 4.1-mile, 37-tower aerial rope tramway was completed to haul ore from the Triumph Mine west through Elkhorn Gulch, across the highway to a railroad siding just south of the Elkhorn Road for shipment out of the valley. It could handle 20–32 tons of ore per day. Ore was previously hauled to the railroad siding by truck. In the 1950s, the tramway was disassembled and sent to Salt Lake City.

Ketchum's Main Street was busy with cars and horse-drawn vehicles during a Fourth of July celebration in 1924.

This photograph, taken in 1925, shows Ketchum's train station looking northwest toward Griffin Butte. The vacant land around the depot was owned by the Ketchum Livestock Association and was used to hold sheep waiting for shipment.

In 1929, Charles Brandt built Bald Mountain Hot Springs Lodge on Ketchum's Main Street with 31 tourist cabins and a 200,000-gallon natatorium, spending $100,000, which included $50,000 to build an underground pipeline to bring hot water from his Guyer Hot Springs Resort to the lodge. Count Schaffgotsch stayed at the lodge when he was looking for a place for Harriman's ski resort, as did Union Pacific personnel when Sun Valley was being built.

Many Ketchum children learned to swim in Bald Mountain's pool filled with Guyer Hot Springs water. The Brandts sold the lodge in 1964. It continued in operation, although the pool closed in 1988. In 1996, the site was purchased for development. The Aspen Ski Corporation built the four-star Limelight Hotel, which opened in December 2016.

Ketchum's Main Street is pictured in the early 1930s. Griffith Grocery Store is on the left, built by I.I. Lewis in 1884, and Lane Mercantile is on the far right. There was not much traffic in those days.

Griffith Grocery on Ketchum's Main Street, shown here in the mid-1930s, was operated by Al and Oscar Griffith, sons of Ketchum pioneer Al Griffith. This was one of the two buildings erected by I.I. Lewis in 1884. It was most recently the Cornerstone Restaurant and is now the home of the Ketchum Culinary Institute.

The Ketchum Kamp Hotel, on the east side of Ketchum's Main Street, offered gambling and a few rooms to rent. It became the Casino and is still in operation.

The town of Galena was abandoned during the 1890s, but its store continued to sell provisions. In 1923, Charles and Pearl Barber purchased the store, sold gas and provisions, and rented cabins. In 1976, it became a cross-country skiing area. The Blaine County Recreation District later turned Galena into a major cross-country skiing and mountain biking facility.

The Comstock & Clark building, at Ketchum's Main Street and what later became Sun Valley Road, was bought by Jack Lane in 1920. It became Lane Mercantile, a place where sheep men met to socialize and conduct business.

When Sun Valley was being built, Lane Mercantile became the phone booth and impromptu resort office for the builders and railroad officials, according to Sun Valley publicist Dorice Taylor. "If you weren't invited upstairs to the Lane kitchen for a drink you didn't rate." Sun Valley was practically built there, since there was nowhere else in town to sit down, and it had a phone.

From 1933 to 1942, the Civilian Conservation Corps spent $3 billion and employed 3.4 million men to work in the country's forests and parks. The CCC gave significant assistance to the country's fledgling skiing industry by cutting trails and building facilities.

Workers from the CCC camp in Warm Springs (shown in 1933) did extensive work in the valley, creating trails, building bridges, and working on numerous other projects. Alf Engen directed CCC and Forest Service crews as they cut new ski runs on Bald Mountain in 1938 and 1939.

Seven

THE UNION PACIFIC OPENS SUN VALLEY IN 1936

Averell Harriman was the son of E.H. Harriman, one of the country's wealthiest men from his control of the Union Pacific Railroad. In 1932, in the middle of the Great Depression, Averell became Union Pacific board chairman after the railroad industry "collapsed like a rotten trestle" and passenger traffic was decimated, according to Maury Klein in *Union Pacific*.

In 1935, Harriman came up with a revolutionary idea. Although skiing was just a fledgling sport, the Union Pacific would build a destination ski resort to increase passenger traffic and add luster to winter rail travel. Harriman sent Count Felix Schaffgotsch from Austria to tour the West to find the best location. Schaffgotsch toured six states in six weeks, rejecting many areas that later became successful ski resorts—either their snow conditions or locations were unacceptable. Ready to give up, the count was told by a Union Pacific employee about Ketchum, an old mining town on a branch line that cost more to keep clear of snow than any except its Yellowstone line.

Schaffgotsch explored the area around Ketchum in February 1936, concluding it had the perfect combination of snow, weather, and hills. He told Harriman it was the perfect place, with "more delightful features for a winter sports center than any other place I've seen in the United States, Switzerland or Austria." Harriman visited Ketchum, "fell in love with the place then and there," and began a fast track project to build a ski resort to open by Christmas 1936.

The Union Pacific bought the 4,000-acre Brass Ranch outside Ketchum for $39,000. Harriman hired Steve Hannagan, a public relations pioneer known for changing Miami Beach from a mosquito-infested swamp into a playground for the rich. Hannagan hated the cold. He named the resort Sun Valley to downplay its cold and snow and emphasize warmth and created a poster of a skier stripped to the waist, reading "Winter Sports under a Summer Sun." Hannagan developed a plan to promote a high-end resort in Idaho's mountains using celebrities, attractive women, Olympic stars, and monied families. Union Pacific engineers invented the chairlift, based on a system to load bananas onto boats, to carry skiers up mountains quickly and in comfort at a time when skiers had to hike up hills before skiing down.

Sun Valley, built for $1.5 million, opened in December 1936 in the remote mountains of Idaho. It was the country's first destination ski resort and attracted Wall Street barons, the Chicago social set, Hollywood stars, and serious skiers. It offered a luxurious lodge with high-end shops and a ski school with Austrian instructors who made skiing sexy. Sun Valley became the "St.

z of America," and "the most 'in' place to get a suntan this side of Waikiki," according to udy Abramson in *Spanning the Century*. Dick Durrance, Dartmouth's famous ski racer, said Sun Valley was the most important influence in the development of American skiing. It had a monopoly on skiing grandeur for several decades and influenced ski areas that developed later.

Harriman used ski racing to make his new resort an international destination and the country's skiing center. Harriman Cup tournaments were the country's most prestigious and competitive events, attracting the world's best skiers. The 1943 *American Ski Annual* reported: "Just as it is the dream of every tennis player to compete once at Wimbledon, it is every skier's hope to participate in the famous Harriman Cup Races at Sun Valley." US Olympic teams for the 1948 and 1952 games were selected at Sun Valley and trained there afterwards. Best known is Gretchen Fraser, who in 1948 won a gold and silver medal at St. Moritz, the first American to win an Olympic medal in skiing. Sun Valley was a cultural icon that was kept in the nation's eye for decades by major newspapers, magazines, and movies. It was famous for bringing European skiing ambiance to America. Its international influence was illustrated when, in 1950, an Austrian newspaper said that with the help of the Marshall Plan, its Arlberg region could become "Austria's Sun Valley."

Sun Valley was never intended to make a profit. Harriman said, "We didn't run it to make money; we ran it to be a perfect place . . . and the publicity I thought was worth very much more than the deficit." The Union Pacific spent $350,000 to $500,000 a year on the resort. Harriman left the railroad for government work before World War II and never returned. Rail passenger travel continued to decline after the war, and with Harriman gone, the subsidy became harder for the railroad to justify. The Union Pacific had spared no expense to make the resort one of the best in the world, but let it decline after the war. In 1964, the Union Pacific sold Sun Valley to the Janss Company for $3 million, and Bill Janss bought it from his family's company in 1968. Janss made substantial investments in the resort but lacked the money to take it to the next level. In 1977, the Holding family, owners of Sinclair Oil Company, purchased the resort for $12 million and remade Sun Valley into one of the country's premier year-round resorts, restoring its international status.

This is a c. 1905 formal portrait of E.H. Harriman with sons Roland (left) and Averell. E.H. Harriman led a group that bought the Union Pacific out of bankruptcy in 1897, and the railroad became the basis for the family fortune. Averell became Union Pacific board chairman in 1932. He created Sun Valley as a destination ski resort to stimulate passenger travel decimated by the Depression. (Courtesy Idaho Department of Parks and Recreation.)

Valley residents skied as a means of transportation and recreation, using homemade skis, hiking boots, and a single long pole that was dragged between their legs as a rudder to turn and as a brake to slow down. This was not the sport brought to Sun Valley in 1936.

Averell Harriman sent Count Felix Schaffgotsch (shown here) to tour the West in the fall of 1935 to find a location for a destination ski resort. After traveling through six states in six weeks and rejecting many sites that later became ski resorts, in February 1936, he was taken to Ketchum at the end of an old spur line that was more expensive to keep clear of snow than any except the Yellowstone line.

This is how Ketchum looked when Count Schaffgotsch arrived in 1936, looking northwest toward Bald Mountain, Warm Springs Canyon, and Griffin Butte. Ketchum was a small mountain town, virtually deserted in the winter, with most of its businesses closed. However, it had the combination of location, snow, and weather the count wanted. He told Harriman, "this without doubt is the perfect place." (Photograph by Martyn Mallory.)

In March 1936, the Union Pacific bought the 4,000-acre Brass Ranch east of Ketchum, which was the historic Lewis homestead, for $39,000. This photograph looks over the ranch toward Ketchum and Baldy. The Sun Valley Resort was in unincorporated Blaine County, but access to Bald Mountain was through Ketchum. Sun Valley incorporated as a town in 1947.

Averell Harriman hired Charles N. Proctor, a 1928 US Olympian and Boston ski store owner (shown here), and John E.P. Morgan, a financier, to design his resort. In the spring of 1936, they located areas for the resort's ski hills, lifts, and runs, and designed an extensive backcountry skiing system. Harriman named Proctor Mountain after Charles.

Averell Harriman (right) and publicist Steve Hannigan inspect Sun Valley Lodge under construction. It was designed by architect Gilbert Stanley Underwood, known for designing national park lodges. The lodge was concrete, but raw wood was placed on it when wet, making the exterior appear to be wood. Work started in May 1936, and the resort opened in December 1936. Hannagan named the resort Sun Valley and created a plan for its development.

Union Pacific engineer James Curran invented the chairlift based on a system to load bananas onto ships. The system was chosen for use at Sun Valley by Charles Proctor over objections from the railroad's engineering department. It was tested at Union Pacific headquarters in Omaha, Nebraska, using subjects on skis and roller skates. The design of the chairlift was patented and became the standard for ski areas all over the world.

Sun Valley Lodge is seen here in the winter of 1937, before the inn and village were built. The smoke comes from burning coal for boilers to heat the lodge. Three trains a week brought coal from Wyoming and took the resort's dirty laundry to Union Pacific headquarters at Omaha, Nebraska, for washing, since Sun Valley lacked laundry facilities.

Harriman wanted a ski school led by Austrians to teach the Arlberg technique, developed by Hannes Schneider in St. Anton. Count Schaffgotsch (right) hired Hans Hauser (left), a two-time Austrian downhill champion, as its director and five Austrian instructors, giving Sun Valley an international flavor. The ski school began a system of organized teaching in this country.

SUN VALLEY'S FORMAL OPENING DUE ON DEC. 21

$1,000,000 PUT INTO NEW AREA

IDAHO'S NEW SLOPE--AND DISCOVERER

MARCH 5-8 IS TOURNEY DATE

Helen Jacobs Is Made Member Of 'Big C' Society

Colorado Gridders In 'Sugar' Workouts

Unbeaten in Two Years

This Is the Life SKI

For Health and Sports Thrills

COME TO NAT GILBERT

Sales and Showrooms
1114 Aurora Ave. GA. 2010

Leading Makes of SKIS, EQUIPMENT SUPPLIES

For Sale or RENT

Hockey Loses Roth, Famous As 'Iron Man'

The Union Pacific opened its $1.5-million Sun Valley Resort in December 1936 with Hollywood celebrities, New York financiers, and wealthy socialites attending. The resort had all it needed for a spectacular opening except for snow. Nervous Union Pacific executives let everyone stay for free until it arrived. The opening was publicized all over the country, helping to make the resort a cultural icon.

Steve Hannagan's famous ad, "Winter sports under a summer sun," emphasized sun and warmth and not the cold and snow the Florida native disliked. Hannagan designed a plan to make Sun Valley an icon for winter sports and snow, like Florida was for sun, by using celebrities, attractive women, Olympic stars, and monied families. (Courtesy Union Pacific Museum.)

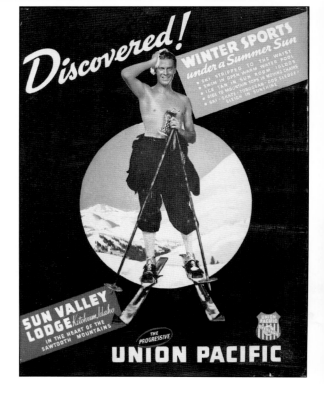

When Sun Valley opened, chairlifts operated on Dollar Mountain, the beginner hill (shown), and on Proctor Mountain, the advanced hill. Bald Mountain had no lifts until the winter of 1940—it was considered too difficult. Backcountry skiing in the surrounding mountains was available for advanced skiers. Lift tickets cost $15 a week, and ski lessons were $3.50 a half-day and $5 for all day.

A skier loads onto the Proctor Mountain chairlift. After chairlifts were built on Baldy for the winter of 1940, Proctor was only used occasionally. In 1951, the Proctor chairlift was moved to Baldy, running parallel to the Roundhouse lift to the summit, which was replaced by a double chairlift in 1958. In 1974, Cordova, Alaska, bought the Proctor chair for $20,000 for Mount Eyak.

Pictured here is Sun Valley Village, the road to the Proctor Mountain chairlift, and the lift extending up the mountain around 1938. Proctor was "an ideal ski mountain, offering every type of terrain and every grade of ski slope," according to Andy Hennig's *Sun Valley Ski Guide*. It had 25 runs, including steep and long, steep and gentle, to the valley floor, and one- or two-mile runs from the top of Proctor.

Passengers could ride Union Pacific trains to Sun Valley, traveling safely and in comfort. First-class travel from Seattle cost $34 round-trip or $12 for a lower berth. Sun Valley became a familiar paradise for Seattleites. The *Seattle Times* said "Sun Valley was 26 hours from Seattle by train, and 20 hours by car, but it might as well be in Seattle's back yard."

In the winter of 1937, *I Met Him in Paris* became the first of many movies filmed at Sun Valley. A set was built at Baker Creek with a Swiss hotel, ice rink, and village, and the movie brought an abundance of free publicity to the resort. *Sun Valley Serenade* is the best-known movie filmed at the resort. Ski school director Friedl Pfeifer said the 1940 movie would "forever change the image of Sun Valley."

Harriman used racing to make Sun Valley the center of US skiing, and Harriman Cup races attracted the world's best skiers. The 1937 and 1938 downhills were held near the present Sawtooth National Recreation Area headquarters (named Durrance Mountain by Harriman). In 1937, Dartmouth's Dick Durrance beat the favorite, Hans Hauser, the Austrian downhill champion and Sun Valley Ski School director. Here, Durrance receives the Harriman Cup from Averell's wife, Marie.

In the summer of 1937, the Union Pacific built the Challenger Inn (now Sun Valley Inn) to accommodate 400 budget-minded travelers and a Swiss-themed village with many stores and services. Crews also built a golf course, rodeo grounds, an opera house, the Trail Creek Lodge, the Harriman chalet, and the Ruud Mountain ski jumping center, and dammed Trail Creek to create a lake and provide irrigation for the resort, all at a cost of over $1 million.

Sun Valley Lodge and Village are seen looking east down Trail Creek toward the Pioneer Mountains. In 1939, the lodge cost $6 to $25 a day and the inn $3 to $7.50. A couple could "manage a thoroughly adequate two-weeks stay in Sun Valley for about $500," according to *The New York Times*.

Summer season was also important for Sun Valley. Ads said it provided a high-end experience, "situated in the beautiful Sawtooth Mountain Range and surrounded by some 25,000 square miles of untouched wilderness," with "tennis courts and outdoor swimming pools, horseback treks through mountains, fishing in lakes and streams rarely visited by the sportsman." (Courtesy Union Pacific Museum.)

In the summer of 1937, the Union Pacific spent $65,000 to build rodeo grounds, "the most modern western sports stadium ever created," according to press releases. There was an 11,000-seat covered grandstand, an open grandstand, and an oval track around them. The first Sun Valley Rodeo was held in August 1937, and rodeos became important parts of summer festivities.

In the summer of 1937, Alf Engen and Sigmund Ruud designed a ski jump on Ruud Mountain (named after Sigmund), allowing Sun Valley to hold four-way competitions (downhill, slalom, cross-country, and jumping). A 40-meter jump was built taking advantage of the hill's natural slope designed for 140-foot jumps. A J-bar leading to the Proctor Mountain chairlift was converted into a chairlift for Ruud, and the mountain became the center for jumping and slalom events.

Alf Engen soars over Ruud Mountain in 1938. Engen was one of the world's best jumpers, winning multiple national championships and setting several national distance records, and one of the best all-around skiers (national four-way champion in 1940 and 1941). He competed for Sun Valley from 1937 to 1948. (Photograph by Charles Wanless; courtesy Alan Engen.)

Skiers could get off Ruud Mountain's chairlift at its midpoint to reach its jump or go to the top to reach the slalom course. The Ruud Mountain ski lift and judge's tower still stand as monuments to the resort's history, recognized by the National Register of Historic Places. (Author's photograph.)

This publicity photograph in Sun Valley Village shows the many activities at the resort. They included riding in a sleigh pulled by reindeer, downhill skiing, sledding, dog sleds, skijoring, ice skating, and cross-country skiing. Sun Valley brought reindeer from Alaska in 1938, training them to haul sleighs to carry guests. They caused problems and were soon returned home.

Averell Harriman said, "No one has really lived . . . until he has skied." Here he is with Gary Cooper, a Sun Valley regular along with Clark Gable, Ingrid Bergman, Ernest Hemingway, and many others. Sun Valley was the most satisfying venture of his career, and skiing replaced polo in his life. As Rudy Abramson noted in *Spanning the Century*, "Harriman fussed over Sun Valley as he had none of his other business enterprises."

Averell's daughter Kathleen was raised amid great wealth and was a prominent figure at Sun Valley. She was on the Bennington College ski team and made the 1940 US Olympic ski team before the games were cancelled. She accompanied Averell to England and Russia during World War II. Her obituary read, "her life is a window into both Gilded Age America and the changing role of American women in the era between the world wars."

This section of a 1938 Sun Valley map shows backcountry skiing northwest of the resort using icons for skiers and snowcats. Farthest northwest (off the map), Baker Creek offered backcountry skiing and skiing during Christmas, when snow was lacking in Sun Valley. Boulder Mountain and Durrance Mountain (site of Harriman Cup downhills in 1937 and 1938) had three runs. Race Mountain had three runs, and Hauser Mountain (named for Hans Hauser, Sun Valley Ski School director) had two. There was skiing on the north ridge of Warm Springs Canyon, accessed through Heidelberg Gulch. Three figures show skiing on "Old Baldy Mountain," one on top, one going down River Run Canyon, and another on Cold Springs Canyon. Several warming huts are shown, including Boulder Mine hut at upper right and Elkhorn cabin at lower right.

This section of the 1938 map shows Sun Valley's lifts on Dollar, Ruud, and Proctor Mountains. A run went from the top of Proctor, along "the Ridge Trail on Elkhorn Ridge," then into Elkhorn basin. A run from the top of Proctor went east toward Uncle John's Cabin and Corral Creek Road; skiers could go to Trail Creek to catch a bus back to the lodge. Snowcat skiing is shown on Corral Creek Run. Pioneer Cabin, an overnight facility, was reached by skis from Corral Creek. There was skiing on the ridge between Elkhorn and East Fork west of Peters Creek. Several warming huts are shown, including Elkhorn Cabin (lower left) and Uncle John's Cabin and Saw Mill Hut at center.

In September 1937, Harriman had snowcats, also known as snow tractors or snow tanks, built for Sun Valley. Designed by the US Forest Service for Mount Hood's Timberline Lodge, they could carry 30 people on grades of 30 to 40 percent at 4 to 8 miles per hour and go 20 miles per hour downhill. They took skiers into backcountry skiing locations beginning in the winter of 1938.

In the fall of 1938, Sun Valley built Pioneer Cabin for backcountry skiing in the Pioneer Mountains, eight miles northeast of Sun Valley at 9,500 feet and reached by a five-mile hike that gained 2,400 feet and took several hours. It slept six (enlarged to sleep eight in 1938). Guests were pampered, skiing in the morning, napping in the afternoon, and eating food prepared by Sun Valley chefs.

Harriman had the Union Pacific invest in a fleet of new, fast, high-tech trains called streamliners that revolutionized the industry. This is the *Little Nugget* bar car on the *City of Los Angeles*, a streamliner bringing skiers from New York to Sun Valley for Christmas 1937. The train had the excitement and thrill of a luxury cruise, according to Sun Valley publicist Dorice Taylor.

The 1938 Harriman Cup attracted 54 of the world's best skiers, with women competing for the first time. Here, Dick Durrance finishes the downhill in wet, heavy snow and limited visibility, winning his second cup. He won his third cup in 1940, getting permanent possession of the trophy. Durrance, a member of the 1936 US Olympic team and favorite of Harriman, worked at Sun Valley after graduating from Dartmouth.

Horse-drawn wagons take Sun Valley guests down Ketchum's Main Street in the winter of 1938. The Casino on the right used to be the Ketchum Kamp Hotel. Lane Mercantile is at upper right.

Gambling was tolerated in Ketchum, where a number of popular clubs operated, including the Sawtooth, Casino, Alpine, Tram, Slaveys, Club Rio, and Idaho Club. The Christiania on Sun Valley Road offered high-stakes gambling. Managed by Dutch Weinbrenner, allegedly a member of Detroit's Purple Gang, it was rumored that mob money financed the facility, according to Dorice Taylor.

Pat "Pappy" Rogers (pictured with his wife, Peg) was Sun Valley's manager beginning in 1938 and was responsible for creating much of the resort's ambiance. A favorite of Harriman, "under his rule Sun Valley enjoyed its golden years as a resort," according to Maury Klein in *Union Pacific*. His battle with the Union Pacific over its declining subsidy to Sun Valley after World War II led to his departure in 1952.

Friedl Pfeifer was a top Austrian racer who taught for Hannes Schneider at St. Anton. In 1938, he became the director of the Sun Valley Ski School, which he expanded and made more professional. Pfeifer said, "The social whirl that centered around the Duchin Room . . . where an orchestra played every night, made Sun Valley a never-never land where everyone was rich and young and all invited to the dance."

In the fall of 1939, Ernest Hemingway (right) came to Sun Valley, staying at the lodge at the Union Pacific's expense; he wrote part of *For Whom the Bell Tolls* here. Hemingway became close friends with Hollywood regulars, including Gary Cooper (left), and locals with whom he shared a love of the outdoors. Through the late 1940s, Hemingway spent falls and some winters in the valley. He lived in Ketchum from 1958 until he committed suicide there in 1961.

Sun Valley's second backcountry facility, Owl Creek Hut, was built in 1940 eighteen miles north of Ketchum, three miles south of Galena Lodge, and four miles west of the highway. At 8,000 feet, it had good skiing from October to June. It was destroyed by an avalanche in 1952, and its timbers were used to build a warming hut on Baldy.

Three single chairlifts were installed on Bald Mountain for the winter of 1940, greatly expanding the lift-served skiing. The March 21, 1940, *New York Times* reported, "Mile after mile of timberless terrain, four chairlifts that make skiing all downhill and fields of all degrees of descents and constant sunshine make this mountain resort the only one of its kind in North America."

Chair 1, at the bottom of Bald Mountain, loaded passengers on the east side of the Big Wood River, so they rode over the river on their way up the mountain. It was later moved west of the river, and a bridge was built for skiers to walk to the chair.

The Roundhouse, named for a building used in railroad maintenance and repairs, was built at the top of the Exhibition chair, where skiers could eat, relax, and party. The Roundhouse lift took skiers to the top of the mountain. Sun Valley accommodated the wishes of the rich and famous, who could rent the Roundhouse, making it known for wild parties where champagne flowed freely.

Baldy became famous for long cruising runs and glade and bowl skiing. Wendolyn Spence Holland wrote in *Sun Valley*, "With good snow, skiers can feel at one with the soul of skiing. Each of its three canyons offers long, consistent vertical descents. The rounded summit leads down to open, undulating terrain with slopes swooping downward through glades and drainage—without long flat shoulders requiring poling, like so many other flagship mountains have."

In the early 1940s, Sun Valley expanded recreational opportunities for its summer and fall visitors. Silver Creek, 25 miles southeast of Sun Valley near Picabo, was prime territory for hunting and fishing and one of the West's best spring-fed creek fisheries. Sun Valley purchased two ranches there to create Sun Valley Ranch, where Sun Valley hunting guide Taylor Williams (right) and a guest hunt ducks.

Sun Valley closed in December 1942 and served as a naval hospital during World War II, reopening on December 21, 1946. It continued to be the country's primary destination ski resort but faced a changed economic and social scene and never achieved the same status as before the war. In the 1950s, the Union Pacific slashed its subsidy, and the resort began to run down. (Courtesy Union Pacific Museum.)

In February 1946, Gary Cooper (center), Clark Gable (right), and their spouses came to Sun Valley before it reopened, staying at Bald Mountain Lodge. They rented Dollar Mountain to ski, and the resort brought instructor Sigi Engl (left) to town to ski with them.

In December 1946, before Sun Valley reopened, the shah of Iran came to ski, inspired by *Sun Valley Serenade*. Otto Lang took him to an abandoned mining community in Boulder Basin north of Ketchum where an old cabin was fixed up, two new outhouses were built, and they skied using a snowcat. The shah was a good skier and returned several times.

In 1947 and 1948, filmmaker Warren Miller lived in an unheated trailer in a Sun Valley parking lot, becoming the classic ski bum. In 1949, he was hired as a ski instructor, getting free room and board, a ski pass, and $125 a month. Miller made 500 films over 30 years, returning often to Sun Valley to film skiers on Baldy. He said he never ruined a story with the absolute truth.

The 1948 US Men's and Women's Olympic teams were selected at Sun Valley. Before the tryouts, Sun Valley provided free accommodations to promising young racers (40 men and 20 women) coached by Alf Engen. The teams stayed at Sun Valley after they were selected for intensive training with Olympic coaches Alf and Walt Prager (kneeling in the front row).

Members of the 1948 US women's Olympic team pose on Bald Mountain. From left to right are Gretchen Fraser, Andrea Mead, Paula Kahn, and Brynhild Grasmoen. Tacoma's Gretchen Fraser won a gold and a silver medal in the 1948 St. Moritz Olympic Games, the first American to win an Olympic medal in skiing. Fraser also won the American Ski Trophy for 1948, "one of the most coveted of all ski honors," according to *The New York Times*.

After the Olympics, Gretchen Fraser retired from competition, having won 17 championships for the Sun Valley Ski Club and two Olympic medals. She was hired to market Sun Valley, capitalizing on her signature look with her hair in pigtails. Gretchen's Gold Run on Sun Valley's Seattle Ridge is named for her, and the lodge dining room is named Gretchen's. (Courtesy Tacoma Library.)

The US ski teams for the 1952 Olympics in Oslo, selected at Sun Valley, stand in front of the Challenger Inn. Ketchum native Jimmie Griffith (first row, far right) was tragically killed before the games in a training accident. Five of the ten men and five of the eight women were Sun Valley Ski Club members. Gretchen Fraser managed the women's team. (Courtesy the Griffith family.)

After the 1952 Olympics, Sun Valley hired some of the world's best skiers for its ski school. This c. 1953 photograph shows, from left to right, Jack Reddish (1948 and 1952 US Olympic team); Norwegian Stein Eriksen (1952 Olympic gold in grand slalom and silver in slalom); Austrian Sigi Engl (ski school director); and Austrian Christian Pravda (1952 Olympic silver in grand slalom and bronze in downhill). Stein Eriksen performed somersaults every Sunday on Ridge Run.

Christian Pravda, who taught at Sun Valley from 1952 to 1966, races in the 1956 Harriman Cup slalom. Pravda could "go down a hill of extreme bumps and make it look as smooth as a floor," said a fellow ski instructor. Pravda won the Harriman Cup in 1953, 1956, and 1959, the only three-time winner besides Dick Durrance.

In 1952, an avalanche on Lookout Bowl killed four people, including ski instructor Victor Gottschalk. The bowls were closed by the mountain manager because of the amount of new snow, but ski school director Sigi Engl opened them. Over 150 Sun Valley employees and guests searched for bodies using bamboo probes. Three bodies were found, but one remained buried until spring.

Ernest Hemingway and his fourth wife, Mary, returned to Ketchum in 1958 and bought a house that looked east over the Big Wood River toward the Pioneer Mountains in 1959. Hemingway battled depression and medical issues before committing suicide there in 1961. He is buried in Ketchum. His memorial is on Trail Creek, and the Community Library sponsors a yearly Hemingway seminar and manages the Hemingway house.

Airlines and automobiles continued to take away rail passenger service in the 1950s, eroding Sun Valley's role with the Union Pacific, although ski trains continued to be important. The *Snowball Express* ran from Los Angeles between 1958 and 1972, carrying a total of 12,957 skiers directly to Sun Valley and offering orchestras and boxcars where skiers could party the whole trip.

Dorice Taylor, Sun Valley's publicist until the 1960s, saw Sun Valley in its glory days and then its decline after World War II as the Union Pacific cut its subsidy to the resort: "Elegance began to go. . . Times were changing." Sun Valley was sold to the Janss Company in 1964 for $3 million, and the company invested heavily in the resort and revitalized it.

In 1968, Bill Janss (seen here skiing on Baldy in the 1960s) bought Sun Valley from his family's company and expanded it, but he faced increasing competition from new resorts opening all over the West and lacked capital to take it to the next level. In 1977, Janss sold Sun Valley for $12 million to the Holdings, a Utah family with the resources to continue its rebirth.

Palmer Lewis donated one of his family's fast freight ore wagons that had been constructed in the 1880s to Ketchum. Since 1958, Ketchum has sponsored the Wagon Days Parade over Labor Day weekend featuring animal-drawn vehicles. The freight wagon hauled by 20 mules is the featured event. Here, it goes through downtown Ketchum in 1958.

Rail passenger service into the valley ended in 1971, although a weekly freight train continued until 1980. The Union Pacific abandoned the Wood River Branch in 1971. The Blaine County Recreational District converted the roadbed into a trail in the 1980s and 1990s, creating an important resource used for cross-country skiing in the winter and biking, skating, roller-blading, and walking the rest of the year. (Courtesy Evelyn Phillips.)

The Trailing of the Sheep Festival in October, considered by some to be one of the country's best fall festivals, celebrates the legacy of sheep ranching. There are sheepdog trials, cultural events, a fair, and a band of over 1,000 sheep trailed through Ketchum on Sunday. Here, a band of sheep walks down the valley's recreational trail. (Courtesy Mary Austin Crofts.)

In 1977, Earl and Carol Holding, owners of Sinclair Oil and other enterprises, bought Sun Valley from Bill Janss for $12 million. They installed high-speed chairlifts and a gondola, invested in snow making, built new lodges ("ultimate on-hill facilities"), opened a new golf course, and remodeled the Sun Valley Lodge, adding a huge spa and fitness center. Sun Valley has regained international prominence from the Holdings' management.

Sun Valley was *Ski* magazine's 2020 Editor's Choice of Resorts. "History, charm, authenticity, and over 2,000 acres of terrain to explore. . . . This resort has it all. . . . Sun Valley Resort's storied past sets it apart from other resorts. . . . There's magic in Sun Valley." *Ski* magazine readers rated Sun Valley the number-two ski resort in America for the fifth year in a row, giving it an impressive number-one rating in seven categories. The opening of Cold Springs Canyon in 2021 will add "380 acres of expert tree skiing. . . . If there was a ranking for ski history, Sun Valley would be No. 1!" In 2019, Ketchum was named the Best Small Town in Idaho by *Insider*, and *Travel+Leisure* listed Sun Valley Lodge as one of "15 Festive Hotels That Make the Holiday Season Even More Magical." (Courtesy Sun Valley Company.)

BIBLIOGRAPHY

Abramson, Rudy. *Spanning the Century: The Life of W. Averell Harriman, 1891–1986.* Chapel Hill, NC: William Morrow and Company, 1992.

Bancroft, Hubert Howe. *History of Washington, Idaho and Montana, 1845–1889.* San Francisco, CA: The History Company, 1890.

"The Depression Arrives Early," from "Idaho, A Century of Pioneers." *Idaho Statesman* Centennial Edition, July 1, 1990.

Griffith, Mary Jane. *Early History of Ketchum and Sun Valley: The Legacy of Al Griffith, A Pioneer and Lifelong Resident.* Ketchum, ID: self-published, 2018.

Hennig, Andy. *Sun Valley Ski Guide.* Omaha, NE: Union Pacific, 1948.

Historic Mines of Blaine County, Idaho. US Bureau of Land Management Shoshone District and the Blaine County Centennial Commission.

History of Idaho Territory: Showing its Resources and Advantages. Wallace W. Elliot & Co., 1884, reprinted Ye Galleon Press, 1973.

The History of Richfield, Idaho, "The Biggest Little Town in Idaho." compiled and edited by Alice Crane Behr and Maureen Hancock Ward, 1995.

Holland, Wendolyn Spence. *Sun Valley: An Extraordinary History.* Ketchum, ID: The Idaho Press, 1998.

Klein, Maury. *Union Pacific: The Rebirth, 1894–1969.* New York, NY: Doubleday & Company, 1989.

McLeod, George A. *History of Alturas and Blaine Counties, Idaho.* Hailey, ID: The Hailey Times, 1930.

Miller, Victoria. *History of the Triumph, Independence and North Star Mines, Blaine County, Idaho.* Idaho Geological Survey, Staff Report 97-1, March 1994.

Randall, Alice Evelyn. *The Effect of the Silver Purchase Act of 1934 on United States, China, Mexico and India.* MBA thesis, Boston University, 1936.

Spence, Clark C. *For Wood River or Bust: Idaho's Silver Boom of the 1880s.* Moscow, ID: University of Idaho Press, 1999.

Strahorn, Carrie Adell. *Fifteen Thousand Miles by Stage.* New York, NY: Putnam's Sons, 1911.

Strahorn, Robert E. *The Resources and Attractions of Idaho Territory.* Bellevue, ID: Idaho Legislature, 1881.

DISCOVER THOUSANDS OF LOCAL HISTORY BOOKS FEATURING MILLIONS OF VINTAGE IMAGES

Arcadia Publishing, the leading local history publisher in the United States, is committed to making history accessible and meaningful through publishing books that celebrate and preserve the heritage of America's people and places.

Find more books like this at
www.arcadiapublishing.com

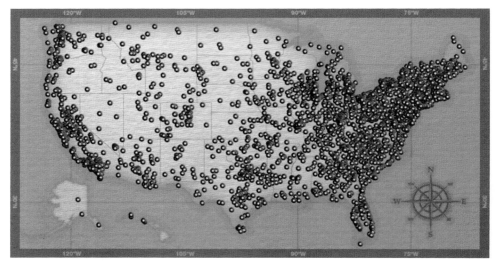

Search for your hometown history, your old stomping grounds, and even your favorite sports team.